Accomack County, Virginia Court Order Abstracts

1676-1678
Volume 5

JoAnn Riley McKey

HERITAGE BOOKS
2011

HERITAGE BOOKS
AN IMPRINT OF HERITAGE BOOKS, INC.

Books, CDs, and more—Worldwide

For our listing of thousands of titles see our website
at
www.HeritageBooks.com

Published 2011 by
HERITAGE BOOKS, INC.
Publishing Division
100 Railroad Ave. #104
Westminster, Maryland 21157

Copyright © 1997 JoAnn Riley McKey

All rights reserved. No part of this book may be reproduced or transmitted in any form or by any means, electronic or mechanical, including photocopying, recording or by any information storage and retrieval system without written permission from the author, except for the inclusion of brief quotations in a review.

International Standard Book Numbers
Paperbound: 978-0-7884-0733-8
Clothbound: 978-0-7884-8945-7

This book is for my daughter

Melanie McKey

INTRODUCTION

Accomack County's fifth book of court orders encompasses only two years and 157 manuscript pages, about half the size of the other court volumes. Beginning in April 1676, and ending in May 1678, these pages document Accomack County's involvement in Bacon's Rebellion and further our understanding of everyday concerns in the 1670's.

Bacon's Rebellion

In 1677, an anonymous author, possibly a man named Cotton of Aquia Creek, wrote a report of Bacon's Rebellion, which had shattered the peace the year before.[1] According to this colonial writer, Nathaniel Bacon, son of Mr. Thomas Bacon of Freestone-Hall in the county of Suffolk, had resided for about three years on a plantation named Curles on the upper part of the James River. Around the beginning of March 1675/76, the Indians killed some Englishmen, including a servant belonging to Bacon. To avenge the death and other damages caused by the Indians, Bacon, without the Governor's consent, "furiously took up arms" against the Indians, putting them to flight. The Governor sent out a company of soldiers to stop him, but Bacon "persisted in his revenge" and instead requested a commission from the Governor. Denied a commission by a messenger, Bacon headed to Jamestown, where, pursued by the Governor's forces, he eventually surrendered himself prisoner.

After a conference with the Governor, Bacon was freed and was "partly promised" a commission as a general against the Indians. However, when the promise was withdrawn, Bacon, whose "mind seem'd mightily to be displeas'd", returned to his rebellion. With his own servants and slaves and the aid of local inhabitants, he attacked and killed about seventy Indians. After the subsequent two day fight, Bacon made an "honourable retreat homewards."

When it was reported that he was "kept close prisoner" in Jamestown, about 800 to 1000 residents of Charles City, Henrico and New Kent Counties marched to his rescue; Bacon quieted them at the Governor's request. When it was clear that he would not receive a commission to fight the Indians, Bacon secretly left Jamestown about the 25th of June 1676. About a week later with four or five hundred men of New Kent County, he marched on Jamestown and drew up before the House of State to demanded a commission from the Governor, the council and the burgesses, who were there assembled. In the face of this threat, the Council and Burgesses obtained for Bacon a commission for one thousand men to go against the Indians along with several other considerations. During the ensuing months "several brushes" between Bacon and the Governor's forces occurred. All able-bodied men were "forc't to take up arms for security of their own lives, and no one reckoning their goods, wives, or children to be their own, since they were so dangerously expos'd to the doubtful accidents of an uncertain war." The rebellion disintegrated soon after Bacon died of natural causes (although some claimed he died from hard drinking).

Residents of the Eastern Shore held divergent opinions about the troubles on the other side of the Chesapeake Bay: Charles Scarburgh and William Kendall[2] were later fined for making statements supportive to Bacon. Col. Stringer, Col. Littleton, and Mr. Foxcroft were mentioned as loyal to the Governor. In December 1676, Daniel Jenifer was specifically honored for his loyalty during the rebellion. Major General John Custis provided a refuge for the Governor himself, when he was forced to flee Jamestown.[3]

When Governor Berkeley fled to the Eastern Shore, some inhabitants at first held themselves aloof, but when pressed by Berkeley for support, they began to bargain; "...instead of the people receiving him with open arms, in remembrance of the former services he had done them, they began to make terms with him..."[4] In their written grievance, the justices claimed that the rebellion had caused great expense and loss of crops because residents had to watch the shore to keep the rebels from invading "our coast, where we had received into our protection the bodies of the right honorable Sir Wm. Berkeley and several other good and loyal subjects of His Majesty fled to our parts from the fury and rage of the said Bacon." They claimed to know of no reason for the rebellion, stating that "some or all of us did protest against his actions as rebellious." They requested that Berkeley remain as Governor and stated that for their loyalty, Berkeley had promised that the Eastern Shore would be free from taxes for 21 years. They also requested to be excluded from paying any costs associated with the rebellion and to be relieved of quitrents.

In the court records themselves, the first indication of trouble came in May of 1676, when Governor Berkeley authorized Col. Wm. Kendall and Capt. Southy Littleton to collect "fort duties" in Accomack County. Ships were required to pay duties in ammunition for the defense of the county.

During 1677 and into 1678, the Accomack County court records contained several references to the rebellion; the petitions generally related to payment for services performed by various citizens and documented the involvement of individuals. Nath. Walker had commanded Jno. Stratton's shallop against the rebels, and in September 1676, had lost the boat at Warrwick's Creek Bay. Jno. Charles requested to be paid for his service from 11 October 1676 to 11 January 1676/77; he had assisted the wounded brought across the bay to Henry Reade's house. Many, like Pawl Carter, Jno. Sturges and Timothy Coe provided meat, salt, butter and cheese. Thomas Evans spent nine days in a shallop under Littleton, nine days in a sloop and two days guarding prisoners. Maj. Jno. West petitioned on behalf of himself and 44 men who served for 34 days under Berkeley's command at Jamestown.

A notice from the new Governor was also recorded. Anyone concerned with the rebellion was prohibited from bearing arms by a proclamation of Governor Jeffries in June 1677.

The Court

All housekeepers and freeholders were ordered to appear at the courthouse at Pungoteage on 16 December 1677, to vote on a convenient place for the removal of the court house. John Cole, the tavern keeper, was quick to remind the court that since his arrival in Pungoteage, he had given them free liberty to hold court at his house, for which he had not charged the county. He went on to say that he had purchased William Freeman's plantation, which he felt was a convenient place to build the courthouse. If this location was selected by the voters, Cole promised to provide 30,000 bricks and timber from the land for the courthouse's construction. He further promised to set up temporary quarters for the court and provide accommodations for those attending court sessions. While no formal acceptance of the offer is recorded, it seems likely that court did soon move to this location, now the town of Accomac.[5]

The same month that the removal of the courthouse was under discussion, the court faced other problems. The commission had been "very much altered," with several magistrates removed "from their ancient places." In November 1677, Governor Jeffries had recommissioned all the justices except for Thomas Browne, Thomas Riding, John Wallop, and John Wise; nor was any mention made of John Custis, who had provided refuge for the Governor during the rebellion. Because of the turmoil, several magistrates refused to sit in court. Charles Scarburgh and Jno. West, claiming that it was all a mistake, requested Jno. Custis to entreat the Governor to send a new commission "according to everyone's ancient place."

In February 1676/77, the financial problems of two women found their way into the court records.

Sarah Painter complained that while her husband, Richard, was absent from the county, his creditors procured an attachment against Painter's estate and goods, including the clothes belonging to Sarah and her children. The court considered her plight and ordered that she retain her bedding and necessary clothing for herself and her children.

Recently widowed by Phillip Ocahone's death, Jone Ocahone had petitioned the Governor. When she married Phillip, she was possessed of a good estate left her by her fist husband, Walter Tayler. But her latest husband had wasted her estate and run into debt, financially ruining Jone and her children. Saying that "Phillip, for his felonious and rebellious actions, having justly suffered death", Jone complained that she was unjustly prosecuted and sued by Phillip's creditors. She implored the Governor to grant clemency and command everyone to desist from suing her for any debts contracted by Phillip Ocahone. Governor William Berkeley granted her request and declared that she should enjoy the estate in her possession.

Assault

An interesting variety of assaults occurred in the two years covered by these records. Wm. Simons, a servant of Edm. Scarburgh, had often bragged that he would strike Richard Jones, Sr., his overseer. The opportunity came when Jones hit Simons, who then "rose up and furiously assaulted" his overseer. After fighting for about an hour, the overseer won; Simons was ordered to serve an extra year.

The discussion of another assault case seems to indicate that the court held evening sessions; on 20 February 1677/78, Arthur Frame was taken into custody for an assault perpetrated "last night" against Benjamin Aires, a public officer, whom the court had sent to preserve the peace (in the tavern, no doubt). Frame was released after apologizing and saying he didn't know Aires was a public officer.

Another night-time assault occurred in Mrs. Charleton's home; it was a completely dark April night when George Russell heard Mrs. Charleton and her maid make "a great crying out." The next morning, Mrs. Charleton's arm was black and blue. Mary Windham, who was known to hold the stick when her mistress was trying to correct her, later petitioned for her freedom; instead she was ordered to pay 50 lbs tobacco for molesting her mistress.

Wm. Tayler, Sr., was called to answer for his assault on Masseteage and his wife, Indians belonging to Occasonson; Tayler's own servants testified to the beatings. After Tayler accused the Indians of killing his hogs, the complaints from both sides were dismissed, as was Tayler's petition to be paid for the testimony his servants had given for the Indians.

No stranger to assault accusations, Lt. Col. John Tilney was sued for assaulting Alexander Gibson with a tobacco stick. Tilney and Gibson had been "capping verses"; one of them would quote a verse and the other would try to cap it with by quoting another verse beginning with the initial letter, final letter, rhyming word, etc. Apparently having met his match, Tilney began to quarrel and ordered Gibson out of his house. In a growing rage, Tilney struck Gibson several times; while Gibson was stooped over, Tilney picked up a tobacco stick with both hands and struck Gibson "a great blow" on his back. Tilney was found guilty and was ordered to pay 500 lbs tobacco to Gibson.

Defamation

Speech was not free in the 1670's; any derogatory comments could come with a price. In July 1676, at the height of Bacon's Rebellion, Jno. Watts, cooper, and Jno. Hanning were taken into custody for speaking words derogatory to the Governor's honor.

While at Cole's tavern, Henry Read commented that Maj. John West had been as big a "rook" as anyone in the country, and might still be. The court found that West had been "damnified to the value of ten pounds tobacco."

In February of 1676/77, Wm. Morgan confessed in court that he had abused Jno. Stratton in his absence by saying he had killed a calf. That same month at an election of burgesses, Stratton called Col. Southy Littleton a mutineer and used other disparaging words in the hearing of several persons. Several months later, after a lawsuit, Stratton apologized and agreed to pay court charges.

Edward Revell suffered the abuse of bad words and language from Nathaniel Bradford, whose apology was recorded on 20 February 1677/78; apparently having learned little from the experience, the next day Bradford used profane language in court and was fined 50 lbs tobacco.

During a discussion of hogs and hog stealing, Hendrick Wagaman reported that Charles Scarburgh had twice caught William Silverthorne in the act of stealing his hogs. Wagaman even quoted Scarburgh's warning: "This is twice I have ketcht you stealing my hogs, but beware the third time." Wagaman, who refused to reveal the source of his information, was sued by Silverthorne.

Disturbances

With the court sessions held at a tavern, one would expect more instances of intoxication than actually appeared. Nathaniel Bradford sued Christopher Sadbury for accusing Bradford of stealing malt and other goods, but when Sadbury was called into court he was too drunk to answer the suit. Sadbury was fined 50 lbs tobacco for his intemperance; his apology at the next court resulted in the dismissal of the original suit.

When Thomas Edge misdemeaned himself in court, James Euell (Edge's security) was ordered to build a new pair of stocks or pay 400 lbs tobacco.

The underlying argument was not recorded, but in November 1677, Dorothy Watts was bound over for breaking the peace against Rebecca Benston. When Dorothy stood by her story, she was acquitted.

Economy

Twice each year the court was to set the prices paid by the innkeeper for liquor; if the prices recorded were any indication, the tobacco based economy must have been quite volatile. In June of 1677, Spanish wine was 100 lbs tobacco per gallon; brandy along with French and Portuguese wines, 80; and rum, 60. By November of that same year, the prices for everything except brandy were exactly half of what they had been five months before. In other transactions, cider sold for 18 lbs tobacco per gallon.

Other costs remained more constant. In April of 1676, a man and his wife each received 50 lbs tobacco per day for attendance at court as witnesses. Later, others consistently received 40 lbs for testifying.

Other costs associated with the court were considerably more expensive. The fine for ignoring a jury summons was 350 lbs tobacco. John West encountered opposition when he requested 3000 lbs tobacco, what he considered reasonable pay for charges in being elected a burgess to the March 1676/77, assembly.

In November 1677, the court repealed the 200 lbs tobacco bounty paid to Englishmen for killing wolves, bears, wildcats and panthers. Interestingly, Indians were still to be paid 150 lbs tobacco for killing the above predators.

According to a witness to the transaction, Edward Hamond sold his plantation for 13,500 or 14,000 lbs tobacco and ten yards of blue linen. Ambrose White received 40,000 lbs tobacco for a 700 acre plantation at Pungoteage. The survey of 300 acres cost one landowner 500 lbs tobacco. A sloop's owner charged 1800 lbs tobacco rent for the use of his boat for one month. In April 1676, Nathaniel Bradford was to pay 3000 lbs tobacco for a Negro woman; the seller was to give him "an assignment for five years and ever after, if he could keep her."

The charge for caring for a child for one year was 1300 lbs tobacco. The same amount was demanded by Peter Pritchet, who at his house, had cared for a mariner named Joseph Jackeill and then had financed his funeral expenses. For the same funeral, Mr. Henry Parke petitioned to be paid 400 lbs tobacco for preaching the sermon.

A merchant named Samuel Sandford sent a cargo worth more than 347 pounds sterling to Virginia with Samuel Cooper, who was to sell the goods in Accomack County. There seems to have been no lack of eager buyers, but Cooper's bookkeeping was questionable, and when he did not make the expected profit, Sandford sued him and demanded an accounting.

Food and Household Items

Articles of food, besides beef and pork, mentioned in these records included Indian corn, peas, butter, cheese, salted meat, malt and walnuts. The wealthier colonists could wash their food down with imported wines, or brandy, sometimes sweetened with a pound of sugar per gallon. Less expensive was rum, and cheapest of all was cider.

When the colonist went home, he might make himself comfortable with a "red shag rug", prop himself up on a hair pillow or a leather feather pillow and rest on a couch with a hide back and bottom. His home would likely contain trunks and chests and possibly cloth, white or dyed a vivid red.

Personal possessions were highly valued, and damages were not taken lightly. Jane Broade immediately realized the gravity of the situation when she accidentally broke the leg from a large pot that she was rolling from the servants' quarters to the "great house." Seventeen-year-old Patience Thornton watched while Jane picked up the broken foot and "fell acrying." Jane cried that she was undone and would be hanged "for I have broken the pot foot." Indeed, John Stratton took poor Jane to court and sued her for the pot, but the court determined that there was no cause for action, the damage being accidental; Stratton had to pay court costs.

Illness

While a specific disease is not mentioned, James Senior, master of the ship *Grossers Adventure*, and his mate, Joseph Jackeil, both died shortly before the court held in May 1678. They are mentioned in the court records only because they left estates and expenses behind.

Other illnesses seemed to be of a less fatal nature. Thomas Bushall promised Dr. Andrew Winter 600 lbs tobacco, three pounds sterling or the value in goods if Winter would take Bushall on as a patient. Winter consented only if a convenient place and a good nurse could be found. Bushall procured a place at Robert Huit's, where Winter cared for him. Although Bushall recovered, he was not a grateful patient. Perhaps it was the bill for 793 lbs tobacco that caused Bushall to make rude and derogatory comments about Dr. Winter's legitimacy.

George Boyes (Boice), who already owed William Stevans 500 lbs tobacco, asked to borrow more and wanted Stevans to "salivate" him. When Stevans complained that he did not have a convenient house, Boyes bargained unsuccessfully with Henry Reade, whose home had been used as a hospital for men wounded in Bacon's Rebellion. Boyes claimed that he had been treated by many surgeons, but that Stevans had done more good than the rest.

John Watts, planter, suffering from an undescribed complaint, had no such praise for his doctor. He sued Dr. John Best, who had neglected Watts as a patient by not coming to treat him for more than six weeks. Testifying to the doctor's long absence was a worker at Watts' house named Will Aleworth; over 50 years old and lame, he also was waiting to consult the doctor. When Robert Watson dropped by, Watts inquired about the doctor and said, "Pray, if you see him, ask him what he mindeth to do, to leave his patient so long in such a sad condition." When he went to church in Pungoteage, Watson sought out the doctor, who commented that Watts must be "fluxed." Then turning the conversation to his own health, Watson complained about being "troubled with the foul disease...and hath been thus twenty years."

Indians

The residents of Accomack County had interactions with the Indian population, but these contacts contrasted sharply with the Indian troubles associated with Bacon's Rebellion on the Western Shore. Indians on the Eastern Shore sometimes were servants to the whites, but they also drank with them in their taverns, sued them in the courts, bargained to pay rent for room and board, and paid tribute.

James, an Indian also known as Winsewack, was a servant to Mr. Robert Huchinson, who apparently allowed James considerable liberty. Wanting to buy something to drink on a court day, James tried to bargain with George Boice to give him credit, promising some pipes in return. Boice refused, saying the last pipes were rotten, and the insults started to fly. When the Indian dared Boice to strike him, the situation degenerated into a fight. After watching James being kicked about the house and pulled by the hair, Alexander Dun urged James to fight, telling him to strike Boice again. This encouragement did not go unnoticed; the two then fought "a good while."

An Indian named Dick bargained to live with Christopher Thomson, who asked three barrels of corn and 200 lbs tobacco for meat, drink, lodging and washing. After the bargain was made, Dick, who said not to bother about the washing, accepted a bottle of brandy from Thomsom, who asked him to be careful with the bottle.

Another Indian named Arthur complained to the court that Roger Miles had kept his gun. Miles was ordered to deliver the gun "well-fixed" to Arthur and pay court costs.

In May 1678, John Cole was granted a certificate for the next assembly; he had presented an account for 288 lbs tobacco delivered by John Custis to the Indians when they brought in their tribute, sixteen gallons of cider.

On the Home Front

Nicholas Laurence turned his wife Mary out of doors and refused to support her. While the court ordered that Mary return to him, they also ordered the church wardens to see that she and her child did not perish from want. If it turned out that Nicholas had no regular residence, the church wardens were to hire him out to support his family.

Before widow Elinor Leatherbury married Capt. Edm. Bowman, she alienated her estate, intending it for her children. This was widely known, for Bowman often "complained" of a hard bargain in marrying a woman with nothing; he claimed it was a demonstration of pure love. While his love for Elinor may have been pure, it did not extend his step-children. After Elinor died, Bowman stood accused of taking several items from the estate intended for her children.

Other children maneuvered out of their inheritances included sixteen-year-old William Fawset, whose own mother seems to have been involved in cheating him. In April of 1675, Widow Rhody Fawset and John Cropper had been accused of fornication, and the court was convinced that she and Cropper "do indecently accompany together."[6] Two years later nineteen cattle belonging to the Fawset estate had been driven to Maryland by Cropper; young William filed a complaint against his own mother and Cropper.

The high mortality of the times left many of orphans, who, if their estates were meager, found themselves in servitude. Orphan Ann Coulston proved in court that she had served her time and won her freedom from William Chace, her master. Born on the other side of the Bay, John Baker was a lame and homeless orphan when John Cole requested permission of the court to put him to work. In exchange for food, drink, shelter, clothing and treatment for his lame leg, Baker agreed to serve Cole for three years.

The case of the Eborne children illustrates the trauma that some children must have endured. After young Sarah Eborne's mother died, her father William Eborne married Mary, who cared for Sarah and bore Eborne three more children. When William died, Sarah was placed in the custody of Joseph Nuton, who wanted the girl to serve him till she was 18 years old. However, Sarah's stepmother, after marrying Thomas Chapwell, successfully petitioned to get Sarah back. Three months later death dealt another blow; Mary Eborne Chapwell died, and while Sarah did not have to return to Nuton, all four children were sent to different homes.

Jon. Hinderson, the son of Gilbert Hinderson, also lost both parents but was somewhat more fortunate. On her death bed, his mother requested that her son be raised by Edmond Joynes, a man also favored by the boy. The court ordered that, until coming of age, Jon. was to remain with Joynes, who in turn could take charge of the estate only if he built a 20 foot square house, planted and tended 100 apple trees, made a cornfield containing 4000 hills of corn, and taught the orphan to read.

Religion

On occasion, citizens were accused of breaking the Sabbath, but rarely to the extent mentioned in April 1678. Thomas Clifton, a member of the grand jury, received a complaint that "one Sabbath day there was very few in the church but at the same time above twenty drinking at Jno. Cole's house the time of sermon."

An unusual example of religious tolerance involved Daniel Jenifer, a wealthy Catholic who actively supported Governor Berkeley during Bacon's Rebellion.[7] Jenifer was appointed sheriff but was not required to take the oath of supremacy; he took only the oath of sheriff.

Such tolerance did not extend to two Quakers, however. In June 1677, George Johnson and Timothy Coe were presented at court for "unlawfully assembling themselves amongst other companies as speakers at Quaker meetings."

Servants

In the two years covered by this court order book, forty-one boys and five girls were brought to court to have their ages judged. Legally determining their ages was necessary because underage servants arriving in the county without an indenture were required to serve until they turned twenty-four. At nine years, William Goulding was the youngest servant; the average age was about fourteen and a half.

Also destined to enter the servant work force at an early age were children surviving the seventeen illegitimate births. Mostly born to servants who were not allowed to marry, these infants sometimes died under mysterious circumstances like the child of Elizabeth Man and Peter Booty, or were farmed out to be cared for by others at the rate of 1300 lbs tobacco per year.

Blaming an "invasion of the spirit that took him up", a servant named Jno. Bacon signed his name as Jno. Smith on a seven-year indenture that he contracted in Bristol, England. If the false name was intended to void the contract, the ruse did not work. The court judged that Bacon should serve out the seven years according to the indenture.

Indebted to his master Thomas Hall and unhappy in his service, Richard Price ran away and sought refuge with John Cropper, a neighbor who illegally fed and hid Price, conspiring with him and offering to trade another servant for him. Found guilty of fraudulently deceiving Hall, Cropper was ordered to pay Price's 1000 lb tobacco debt plus another 300 lbs tobacco. Cropper was apparently allowed to retain Price, who had said he "would never serve Tho. Hall, but would go as far as a pair of shoes would carry him or hang himself first."

John Stephenson, servant to Mathew Scarbrow, must have held the same sentiments. On 26 January 1676/77, he committed suicide in a chamber at Daniel Jenifer's house at Gargaphia by hanging himself with a piece of red cloth edging fastened to one of the chamber window bars.

Thievery

While most complaints of thievery involved animals, other items were stolen as well. Thomas Barnet tried to sell Richard Holland a pigskin saddle, two bridles and three of four loads of high swan shot; Holland, who recognized one of the bridles as belonging to Southy Littleton, wisely refused to bargain with Barnet.

William Custis turned in James Ewel, who apparently had been busy rustling and butchering cattle. A search of his house revealed beef both "hung and green" along with several hides. A neighbor's dog had several times brought home a muzzle, skin or nose of a cow, and once the whole head. Found guilty, Ewel had to pay 500 lbs tobacco to Custis as the informer and another 500 lbs to the county.

John Webster, for "unlawfully carrying away and killing a hog" was ordered to pay 1000 lbs tobacco to the informer and 1000 lbs to the owner.

William Burton, who was both the informer and the owner of an illegally killed hog, was to receive 2000 lbs tobacco from Nathaniel Bradford. Helping to prove Burton's case was Barbery Owen, a 30-year-old woman who had been to Nickowansin to get walnuts. As she was going home, she saw William Burton's sow, which a few days before had been in Owen's pen. Then Barbery heard a gun go off nearby and saw Burton's sow reel and fall down. Thomas Williams came out of the thicket and, placing his foot on the sow, stuck her with his knife. When Nathaniel

Bradford called asking if the barrow was dead, Williams replied that it was a sow.

The court was convinced that Bradford was guilty, but the matter did not end there. Bradford appealed the decision, and both parties sued each other for defamation. When these suits were thrown out, both Bradford and Burton petitioned to have the other taken into custody, which was done.

Winter Weather

Such mundane topics as the weather were generally left undocumented, but the first days of January 1675/76, must have been exceptional. When Jno. Hanson's sloop attempted to enter Nanduy Creek, it lost its anchor at the creek mouth "by extremity of weather." Once in the creek, which was "very much frozen, the sloop remained fast and unmovable in the ice" near Jno. Lecatt's tobacco house. One of the crew was ordered to go ashore and get a stone and wood anchor, which was then to be bound to a new coil of rope that they had in the sloop. Two days later Jno. Lecatt delivered the home-made anchor, but by now the wind was blowing very hard; it had opened the ice and the ship was beginning to move. Tho. Jones, ignoring the anchor, made some sail and ran the sloop aground on Lecatt's shore. There Jones, no doubt exhausted from the cold and the stress, cursed the sloop's owner and went ashore himself.

Names

John Washbourne, the court clerk that recorded these records, had very legible handwriting but, like others of his time, was partial to abbreviations and variations in spelling. In this volume all spellings have been modernized except for proper nouns, which are recorded as originally written.

In addition to the flexible spellings, there is also reason to believe that some given names were flexible as well. Like a parent calling a child by its sibling's name, some records seem to confuse first names among family members. In one apparent error, Jon. Hinderson, who is named as the heir of Gilbert Hinderson, is in the same entry later referred to as "Gilbt." In another case, Sarah Eborne (misspelled "Sarha") was called "Mary," her step-mother's first name. While he was trying to retrieve his dead father's estate, it seems that William Fawset was once mistakenly called John, the name of his father.

The careful researcher will check for every conceivable spelling and keep an open mind regarding various possibilities.

Illiterate citizens made their marks for signatures. As far as possible these marks (or their descriptions) appear in parentheses between the first and last names.

Calendar

Until 1752, Britain used the Roman or Julian calendar. Like their legal counterparts in England, the court in Accomack considered the new year to begin on Lady Day, the 25th of March, which meant that December 1677, was followed by January 1677. To avoid confusion in this volume, dates falling between 1 January and 24 March include both years. A date originally written as 9 January 1677, appears as 9 January 1677/78.

Original Court Orders

These Accomack County court order abstracts were taken from microfilms of the original handwritten documents. Sometimes words were obliterated by ink blots or were otherwise unreadable; a partially legible word of one with a questionable spelling is followed by a question mark. When larger sections were illegible, that fact was noted in brackets.

This book of abstracts is intended as a guide to the original order book. The microfilm copy is known as *Accomack County Orders, 1676-1678*, and is available through interlibrary loan from the Archives Branch, Library of Virginia, 11th street at Capitol Square, Richmond, Virginia 23219.

Introduction Notes

[1] Albert Bushnell Hart, *American History Told by Contemporaries, Volume 1: Era of Colonization, 1492-1689.* (New York: MacMillan Co., 1968), pp. 242-246.

[2] Ralph T. Whitelaw, *Virginia's Eastern Shore: a History of Northampton and Accomack Counties,* (Gloucester, MA: Peter Smith, 1968), pp. 200, 807.

[3] Whitelaw, pp. 109, 1152, 1153.

[4] Susie M. Ames, *Studies of the Virginia Eastern Shore in the Seventeenth Century,* (Richmond, VA: Dietz Press, 1940), p. 9.

[5] Whitelaw, p. 1027.

[6] JoAnn Riley McKey, *Accomack County, Virginia, Court Order Abstracts, 1673-1676, Vol. 4,* (Bowie, MD: Heritage Books, 1997), p. 114.

[7] Ames, pp. 8, 9.

Selected Bibliography

Ames, Susie M. *Studies of the Virginia Eastern Shore in the Seventeenth Century.* Richmond, Virginia: Dietz Press, 1940.

Hart, Albert Bushnell. *American History Told by Contemporaries, Volume 1: Era of Colonization, 1492-1689.* New York: MacMillan Co., 1968.

McKey, JoAnn Riley. *Accomack County, Virginia, Court Order Abstracts, 1673-1676, Vol. 4.* Bowie, Maryland: Heritage Books, 1997.

Webster's New International Dictionary of the English Language, Second Edition, Unabridged. Springfield, Massachusetts: G. & C. Merriam and Co., 1961.

Whitelaw, Ralph T. *Virginia's Eastern Shore: a History of Northampton and Accomack Counties.* Gloucester, Massachusetts: Peter Smith, 1968.

Accomack County Court--18 April 1676

Present: Capt. Southy Littleton   Mr. Richard Bally
             Capt. Richard Hill   Mr. Obedience Johnson (p. 1)

Mr. Robt. Huchinson was foreman of the jury impaneled for this court:

Tho. Birrit	James Collison	Jonathan Owen
Robert Bracye	Tho. Fowks	Robt. Watson
Jno. Brooks	Jno. Hanning	Wm. White
Jno. Care	Thomas Johnson	(p. 1)

Jno. Smith's servant boy named Nicholas Edwards was judged to be 14 years old and was ordered to serve accordingly. (p. 1)

Mr. Tho. Brown entered the court. (p. 1)

Edward Hamond's servant boy named Laurence Gibson was judged to be 14 years old and was ordered to serve accordingly. (p. 1)

Jno. Shepard's servant boy named Jno. Lattimore was judged to be 15 years old and was ordered to serve accordingly. (p. 1)

Jno. Wallop's servant boys were brought to court: Munsly Farsy was judged to be 10 years old, and Tho. Wheeler was judged to be 18 years old. They were ordered to serve accordingly. (p. 1)

Capt. Edm. Scarburgh entered the court. (p. 1)

Mr. Ambrose White's servant boy named Marck Gibson was judged to be 12 years old and was ordered to serve accordingly. (p. 1)

George Brickhouse's servant boy named Richard Smith was judged to be 12 years old and was ordered to serve accordingly. (p. 1)

Mr. Browne exited the court for the following action:
Mr. Thomas Browne's servant boy named Morgan Jones was judged to be 17 years old and was ordered to serve accordingly. (p. 1)

Wm. Tayler's servant boy named Jno. Elliot was judged to be 14 years old and was ordered to serve accordingly. (p. 1)

Capt. Hill exited the court for the following actions:
Capt. Richard Hill's servant boys were brought to court: Solomon Shars was judged to be 10 years old, and Joseph Brickhill was judged to be 17 years old. They were ordered to serve accordingly. (p. 1)

Jno. Lewis' servant named Jno. Allsop acknowledged that he agreed to serve for six years if Lewis would buy him. This was recorded at the request of Lewis. (p. 2)

Mr. Wise and Mr. Custis entered the court. (p. 2)

Tho. Bacy, servant boy of Mr. Jno. Mikell, Jr., was judged to be 15 years old and was ordered to serve accordingly. (p. 2)

At the last court, Tho. Bushall had sued Tho. Willson, who, at this court, answered all points in the complaint. Ordered that the suit be dismissed with Bushall paying court costs. (p. 2)

In the suit of Mr. Jno. Mikell, Sr., against Jno. Coale, the court appointed Mr. Robt. Huchinson and Mr. Wm. Anderson to audit the accounts and report to the court. (p. 2)

On 18 February, an order was passed against Mr. Edm. Bowman as high sheriff in the suit of Amb. White against Jno. Cooke, who failed to answer. Since he failed to produce Cooke, Bowman was ordered to pay the debt of 382 lbs tobacco and court costs. (p. 2)

Jno. Coale sued Wm. Colburne for security for the payment of 878 lbs tobacco. Ordered that Colburne give security for payment by 10 October, and pay the costs of the suit. (p. 2)

Mr. Bally exited and Capt. Littleton entered the court. (p. 2)

Jno. Coale was granted a judgment of 1538 lbs tobacco against Wm. Emot, who was to pay the debt and court costs. (p. 2)

Mr. Custis, Capt. Littleton and Maj. West exited the court. (p. 2)

In his suit against Maj. Jno. West over a debt, Mr. Robt. Huchinson produced an account against West for 579 lbs tobacco. West pleaded the

Act of Assembly for limitation of his accounts and requested the court's judgment. They decided that the account was not pleadable. (p. 2)

Accomack County Court--19 April 1676

Present: Capt. Southy Littleton   Mr. Tho. Riding
            Capt. Charls Scarburgh   Capt. Edm. Scarburgh
            Maj. Jno. West (p. 2)

Tho. Newbold authorized Alexander Swanne to confess a judgment of 2856 lbs tobacco due to Col. Jno. Custis. Signed 18 April 1676, Tho. Newbold. Witness: Wm. Martiall.
Alexander Swan, attorney for Mr. Tho. Nubold, confessed the above debt and court costs. (p. 2)

Wm. Willet was sworn constable for the ensuing year in the precincts formerly served by Wm. Collins. (p. 3)

Maj. West exited the court. (p. 3)

Maj. West petitioned against Mr. Tho. Welburne (attorney: Mr. White) for 1400 lbs tobacco; West alleged that Welburne obliged himself to pay that sum on the account of Miles Grey and requested that the case be referred to Welburne's oath. Since Welburne refused to swear, it was ordered that he immediately pay the sum and court costs. (p. 3)

Isaac Dix (attorney: Charls Holden) petitioned against Jno. Webster (attorney: Mr. Tankard) for "unlawfully carrying away and killing a hog"; Webster confessed. Ordered that Webster pay 1000 lbs tobacco to Capt. Littleton, as the informer for the county, 1000 lbs tobacco to Dix, as the hog's owner, and court costs. (p. 3)

The suit of George Archbold (attorney: Charls Holden) against Capt. Daniel Jenifer (attorney: Mr. Amb. White) was referred to the next court at Jenifer's request. (p. 3)

The suit of Mr. Jno. Mikell, Sr., against Capt. Daniel Jenifer over a debt was referred to the next court at Jenifer's request. (p. 3)

Owen Collonel's servant boy named Jno. Archer was judged to be 18 years old and was ordered to serve accordingly. (p. 3)

Wm. Anderson's servant boy named Richard Saunders was judged to be 17 years old and was ordered to serve accordingly. (p. 3)

Mr. Robt. Huchinson's servant boy named William Waile was judged to be 18 years old and was ordered to serve accordingly. (p. 3)

Edwd. Hamond's servant girl named Ann Meeres was judged to be 17 years old and was ordered to serve accordingly. (p. 3)

Mrs. Rhody Fauset's servant named Joseph Aily was judged to be 12 years old and was ordered to serve accordingly. (p. 3)

Mr. West exited for the following action:
Will: The will of Henry Scarburgh was proved by the oath of George Watson. (p. 3)

George Charnoke was appointed by Alexander Gibson to confess a judgment of 1000 lbs tobacco due to Jno. Coale. Signed 18 April 1676, Alexander Gibson. Witnesses: Joseph Newton and Wm. Martiall.
George Charnok confessed the above debt to Jno. Coale and court costs. (p. 4)

Hendrick Waggaman (attorney: Mr. Tankard) sued Elizabet Gossling (attorney: Charls Holden), but the court found no cause for action. Waggaman was to pay court costs. (p. 4)

Tho. Jones appointed Charls Holden as his attorney in his difference with Mr. Jno. Hanson. Signed, Tho. Jones. Witnesses: Morgin (MT) Thomas and Joseph Green.
The suit of Jno. Hanson against Tho. Jones was referred to the next court at the request of Charls Holden, attorney for Jones. (p. 4)

Wm. Chase confessed a judgment of 565 lbs tobacco and court costs due to Mrs. Ann Boate. (p. 4)

Wm. Chase, who sued Jno. Hanson for 492 lb tobacco, exhibited a bond signed by Hanson in which he promised to hold Chase harmless from the debts of Mathew Pope. Chase made it appear that Mrs. Boate had recovered 450 lbs tobacco and Toby Selvy 42 lbs. Ordered that Hanson pay the debt and court costs. (p. 4)

19 APRIL 1676

Jno. Coale sued Samuel Tayler for 441 lbs tobacco, but Tayler failed to appear. If Tayler failed to appear to answer the charges at the next court, it was ordered that the sheriff pay the debt and court costs. (p. 4)

Mr. Jno. Mikell, Sr., sued Hendrick Waggaman for a debt. At Waggaman's request, the case was referred to the next court. (p. 4)

Hendrick Waggaman, who sued Elizabeth Gossling, did not prove his petition, so a nonsuit and court costs were granted against Waggaman. (p. 5)

Mr. Tho. Welborne sued Jno. Hanning for 430 lbs tobacco, but as there appeared to be no cause for action, the suit was dismissed. (p. 5)

Mr. Tho. Welborne sued Jno. Hanning but did not prove the debt, so a nonsuit and court costs were granted against Welborne. (p. 5)

Mrs. Rody Fawset asked to be released from her bond for good behavior. Proclamation was made three times with no objection against her; she was discharged and paid court costs. (p. 5)

Giles Cope (attorney: Charls Holden) was granted a judgment of 200 lbs tobacco against Jno. Senners (attorney: Mr. Tankard), who was also to pay court costs. (p. 5)

Maj. Jno. West was granted a judgment of 845 lbs tobacco against James Fowks, who was to pay the debt with court costs. (p. 5)

Accomack County Court--20 April 1676

Present: Capt. Southy Littleton
Maj. Jno. West   Capt. Richard Hill
Capt. Edm. Scarburgh   Mr. Richard Bally (p. 5)

The old grand jury was dismissed and the sheriff was ordered to summon a jury for the present year. Mr. Wm. Anderson was named foreman of the following jury:

Jno. Bagwell	Jno. Blockson	Giles Cope
Tho. Barrimore	Jno. Brooks	Isaac Dix
Tho. Barrit	Tho. Burton	Ralph Doe
Tho. Blacklock	Owen Collonell	Edward Dolby

Wm. German	Tho. Johnson	Jno. Prettiman
Mr. George Nickolas	Wm. Major	Jno. Smally
Hack	Mr. Jno. Mikell	Jno. Smith
Tho. Hall	Mr. Roger Mikell	(p. 5)
Rich Holland	Jonath. Owen	

The magistrates were ordered to take an account of the tithables in their precincts as follows:
Mr. Riding: in Hungar's Parish
Mr. Johnson: on the south side of Occahanock
Capt. Edm. Scarburgh: to Mr. Edwar (sic) Revell's Bridge
Mr. Wise: to Deep Creek Mill
Capt. Hill: to the line at Pocomoke
Mr. Jno. Wallop: on the Sea Side down to Gargaphia
Capt. Wm. Custis: to Hungar's Parish. (p. 5)

Capt. Southy Littleton petitioned to be released from his obligation regarding his acting as high sheriff after the death of Mr. Jno. Culpeper. He presented his accounts to the court, which ordered that he have his bond returned to him. The accounts mentioned Richard Kellum but dealt mainly with other fines, levies and fees which totaled 76,270 lbs tobacco. Signed, S. Littleton. (p. 6)

Mr. Tho. Welburne sued Samul. Tayler for 917 lbs tobacco; at Tayler's request the case was referred to the next court. (p. 6)

Ann Oben entered action for a three-year-old heifer against Mathew Ship, who could not be found. Since he did not appear to answer the suit, an attachment was granted against Ship's estate where it could be found in the county. (p. 6)

Mr. Tho. Welburne sued Henry Barnes but did not file his petition according to the law. At Barnes' request a nonsuit with court costs was granted against Welburne. (p. 6)

Mr. Tho. Welburne sued Roger Mikell but did not file his petition according to the law. At Mikell's request a nonsuit with court costs was granted against Welburne. (p. 6)

The court dismissed the suit of Roger Mikell against Mr. Tho. Welburne for a debt, there appearing to be no cause for action. (p. 6)

Maj. Edmd. Bowman had been granted an attachment of 382 lbs tobacco against the estate of Jno. Cook; proclamation was made three times, but no one appeared to bail the attachment. Ordered that the debt and court costs be satisfied with an attached horse in the possession of Arthur Robins and a chest at Maj. Bowman's. (p. 6)

George Dewy was summoned to attend the court as a juryman, but he failed to attend. Ordered that he be fined 200 lbs tobacco and court charges. (p. 7)

Owen Marsh sued Wm. Fletcher for a cow and calf, but Fletcher could not be found. An attachment for the debt and court costs was granted against Fletcher's estate where it could be found in the county. (p. 7)

Capt. Littleton exited the court for the following action:
Capt. Southy Littleton, as assignee of Wm. Sherrwood, sued Wm. Whittington for 800 lbs tobacco, but Whitington failed to appear to answer the charges. Since the sheriff returned Jno. Coale as security for Whittington's appearance, it was ordered that judgment pass against Coale for the debt and court costs. (p. 7)

Capt. Ed. Scarburgh exited the court for the following action:
Capt. Edmd. Scarburgh entered a suit for 3806 lbs tobacco against Edward Hamond, who failed to appear. If Hamond did not appear at the next court, it was ordered that the sheriff pay the debt and court costs. (p. 7)

Deposition of Wm. Nock aged about 32 years: About last March 10, Nock was at the house of Nath. Bradford with Mathew Scarburough when he was asked to witness a bargain between them concerning a Negro woman for whom Bradford was to give Scarburough 3000 lbs of tobacco--half this year and half the next. If three hogsheads would not equal 1500 lbs this year, then Bradford would make it up the next. Scarburgh was to give Bradford a bond saving him from anyone in England or Barbados that might lay claim to the woman. Except for her baptism and the laws of the county, Bradford was to have no security; Scarburgh was to give Bradford "an assignment for five years and ever after if he could keep her." Signed by Wm. Nock, in open court 20 April 1676, before Jno. Washbourne.
The difference was referred to a jury; Mr. Robert Hutchinson their verdict: a bargain existed between plaintiff Mathew Scarburough and defendant Nath. Bradford (attorney: Mr. Amb. White). It was ordered that Bradford pay the 3000 lbs tobacco and court costs.

Bradford requested to appeal to the next general court, which was granted after both parties gave security. (p. 7, 8)

Mr. George Nicholas Hack was granted a judgment of 248 lbs tobacco against Tho. Johnson, who was to pay the debt and court costs. (p. 8)

The suit of Mr. Robt. Huchinson against Jno. West over a debt was referred to the next court at West's request. (p. 8)

Arthur Robins was sworn subsheriff for the ensuing year. (p. 8)

Jno. Brookes swore that he and his wife were summoned as evidences in the suit of Mr. Tho. Welburne against Robt. Bracy and attended four days. Ordered that Welburne pay 400 lbs tobacco and court charges. (p. 8)

Some of the accounts of Jno. Culpeper were recorded. For 1672, the following were mentioned: bounty for one wolf's head (200 lbs tobacco), Tho. Bally, James Harrison, Owen Edmnds., Edm. Kelly, Owen Murfry, Wm. Anderson, Mr. Danl. Jenifer, Mr. David Richardson, Wm. Andrews. Mentioned for 1673: James Harrison, Doctor Abbot, Mr. Revell, Frans. Wharton (for a wolf's head), Simon Foxcroft, Sr., Owen Collonell, Roger Mikell, 3540 lbs as expenses for journeys, Mr. Collison, Mr. Revell, Saml. Tuckfeild, two pipes of wine, Tobby Bull, Morgan Thomas, Wm. Cowdrey, Mr. Upshott, Mr. Sadbury, Wm. Kennett, Wm. Collins, Jno. Rowles, Tho. Johnson, Henry Yardly, Fran. Wharton, Tho. Mattox, David Gibbins. The account was signed by Jno. Coale.

Robt. Hutchinson and Wm. Anderson examined the account between Mr. Jno. Culpeper (deceased) and Jno. Coale and found that 1310 lbs tobacco was due to Coale according to the above records. They desired particulars of two other accounts amounting to 1440 lbs tobacco that Coale also claimed was due. (p. 8, 9)

At the last court Mr. Jno. Mikell, Sr., had sued Jno. Coale for 8476 lbs tobacco. Coale, alleging that he had an account to bring in to balance it, requested the case be referred to this court. The account was audited by Mr. Robt. Huchinson and Mr. Wm. Anderson, who brought in the results; the court dismissed the suit. (p. 9)

Deposition of Wm. Gingee aged about 46 years: In December 1672, Jno. Middelton was transported into this country in the ship *Willing Minde*, commanded by deVron(?). Gingee said that Midleton had a four-year indenture, a copy of which he had seen "enrolled in the office in London." Sworn in open court 19 April 1675, by Wm. Gingee before Jno. Washbourne. (p. 9)

Jno. Motts recorded his desire that Henry Derrick load on the first ship to London or Bristol "all the effects of this parcel and all from George Jnoson" along with anything received from Capt. Littleton. Signed by Jno. Motts. (p. 9)

The Governor of Virginia authorized Col. Wm. Kendall (and in his absence, Capt. Southy Littleton) to collect the fort duties in Accomack County; all ships required to pay duties were to pay in ammunition for "the defence of that Frontier County." Signed by William Berkely and recorded 21 May 1676, by Jno. Washbourne. (p. 10)

The Governor ordered that Maj. Edmd. Bowman be continued as high sheriff of Accomack County for 1676. Signed 21 December 1675, William Berkeley. Recorded 21 May 1676, by Jno. Washbourne. (p. 10)

The Governor appointed Mr. Jno. Wise and Capt. Wm. Custis to the quorum of Accomack County. Signed 22 March 1675/76, William Berkeley. Recorded 21 May 1676, by Jno. Washbourne. (p. 10)

At a general court held at James City on 22 March 1675/76, by the Governor and his council: A petition of the Burgesses of Accomack and Northampton Counties showed that Mr. Jno. Culpeper, sheriff of the counties, received quitrents from both counties in 1673 and 1674. Ordered that after the payment of other public dues, enough of Culpeper's estate be secured to satisfy what he had received as quitrents. Signed by Hen. Hartwell, court clerk. Recorded 21 May 1676, by Jno. Washbourne, court clerk of Accomack County. (p. 10)

Deposition of Jno. Brookes aged about 62 years: Some months ago, Brookes was coming to the court at which Mr. Tho. Welburne sued Robt. Bracy, who was not able to attend. Bracy requested Brookes to tell Mr. Wellburne "that if he would withdraw his action, he would come down and make him satisfaction and pay him what he owed him." Sworn in open court 20 April 1676, by John (IB) Brookes.

Deposition of Jane Brookes aged about 60 years: Said that what her husband declared was the truth. Sworn in open court 20 April 1676, by Jane (O) Broke. (p. 10)

Accomack County Court--1 June 1676

Present: Capt. Southy Littleton   Capt. Edmd. Scarburgh
Capt. Charles Scarburgh   Capt. Rich. Hill
Capt. Wm. Custis   Mr. Richard Bally
Mr. Tho. Riding   Mr. Obedience Jnoson
Mr. Jno. Wallop (p. 11)

Will: The last will and testament of Benjamen Trinniman was probated by the oaths of Tobias Selvy and Elizabeth Selvy. (p. 11)

The "Governor's Remonstrance" was published in open court according to his command. (p. 11)

Accomack County Court--17 July 1676

Present: Capt. Southy Littleton   Capt. Wm. Custis
Capt. Charles Scarburgh   Mr. Tho. Riding (p. 11)

Mr. Robt. Huchinson was foreman of the jury summoned to attend this court:

Mr. Blacklock	Jno. Fenn	Tob. Selvy
Wm. Burton	Mr. George Hack	Abraham Tayler
Jno. Cropier	Tho. Morgan	Wm. Willson
Mr. Jno. Drumond	Jno. Savage	(p. 11)

Mr. Jno. Mickael, Sr., (who married the widow of Mr. Jno. Culpeper) was granted a judgment of 481 lbs tobacco and court costs against Hendrick Waggaman. (p. 11)

Mrs. Tabitha Brown's servant boy named Thomas Bromely was judged to be 15 years old and was ordered to serve accordingly. (p. 11)

Ann Coulston, orphan, petitioned for freedom from her master, Wm. Chace. She proved that she had served according to the Act of Assembly, so it was ordered that she be freed. (p. 11)

Mrs. Tabitha Brown was granted a judgment of 235 lbs tobacco against Edward Hamond. The debt and court costs were to be paid on 10 October. (p. 12)

17 JULY 1676

Mr. Bally entered the court. (p. 12)

Mary Laurence complained that her husband, Nicholas Laurence, "hath turned her out of doors and refuseth her maintenance." Ordered that she return to her husband; the church wardens of Hungar's Parish (the place where they lived) were to take care that Mary and her child did not perish from want. Laurence was to reimbursed the parish and pay court costs. The wardens were to inquire, and if it proved that Laurence had "no certain place of abode, that then they take him up as vagabond and hire him out to maintain himself and family." (p. 12)

Capt. Charls Scarburgh exited the court; Mr. Obed. Jnoson and Mr. Jno. Wallop entered. (p. 12)

Tho. Bushall acknowledged a judgment of 11 pounds 13 sterling due to Mr. Wm. Arriskin. (p. 12)

Capt. Littleton exited the court for the following actions:
Capt. Southy Littleton, on behalf of the county, sued Phillip Hanger for the payment of fort duties. Because Mr. Edw. Revel, Hanger's attorney, showed that Hanger had paid it to Col. Stringer, the suit was dismissed. (p. 12)

The suit of Jno. Harris against Jno. Barnes for 3623 lbs tobacco was referred to the next court at Barnes' request. It had been "so far examined" by the following: Southy Littleton, Rich. Hill, Rich. Bally and Jno. Wallop. (p. 12)

Accomack County Court--18 July 1676

Present: Maj. Jno. West   Capt. Rich. Hill
Mr. Tho. Riding   Mr. Rich. Bally
Mr. Tho. Browne   Mr. Jno. Wallop (p. 12)

Mr. Jno. Wise's servant boy named Wm. Goulding was judged to be 9 years old; he was ordered to serve accordingly. (p. 12)

Mr. Wise entered the court. (p. 12)

Jno. Harris acknowledged a judgment of 3000 lbs tobacco and court costs due to Jno. Coale. (p. 12)

Mr. Jno. Hanson sued Mr. George Nichol Hack; upon balancing the accounts, it appeared that Hack owed 56 lbs tobacco to Hanson. Ordered that Hack pay the debt and court costs. (p. 12)

In the suit of Mr. Wm. Anderson, attorney of Mr. Tho. Welburne, against Robt. Bracy for a debt, the court ordered that the suit be suspended till Welburne or Capt. Waterland could appear "for the more legal determination thereof." (p. 13)

At the last court a fine for 350 lbs tobacco was passed against George Due for ignoring his summons to serve on the jury. Due petitioned for remission, claiming his wife was sick and that he had no contempt of authority. The former judgment was reversed with Due paying court charges. (p. 13)

Mr. Wm. Anderson, attorney for Mr. Tho. Welburne, entered a suit for 999 lbs tobacco against Wm. Colburne, who failed to appear at court. If Colburne failed to appear at the next court, the judgment would pass against the sheriff. (p. 13)

Wm. Cowdry sued Jno. Harris but did not file a petition; a nonsuit was granted against Cowdry, who was also to pay court costs. (p. 13)

Mrs. Ann Boate sued Henry Read, but there appeared to be no cause for action. A nonsuit was granted against Boate, who was also to pay court costs. (p. 13)

Deposition of Joseph Thorne aged about 30 years, 13 July 1676: Thorne was at the house of Mr. Robt. Huchinson about 25 March when he heard Henry Bradford say to Jno. Reeves, "[I] brought [you] in for the term of four years and no more and had sold [you] but for four years and no longer should serve, and if Nath. Bradford had an assignment from [me] for any longer time, [I] will give him his ear." Sworn in open court before Jno. Washbourne, signed, Joseph (J) Thorne.

Deposition of Thomas Williams and Sarah Sadbury: Thomas and Sarah said the same as Joseph Thorne. Sworn in open court before Jno. Washbourne and signed, Thomas (T) Williams, Sarah (SS) Sadbury.

Jno. Reeves, servant to Nath. Bradford, petitioned for his freedom and made it appear that Henry Bradford had brought him in and sold him for only four years. Reeves alleged that he had served beyond that time, but Nath. Bradford claimed the right to five years service. Ordered that the case be referred to the next court where Bradford was to prove his claim or judgment would proceed against him. (p. 13)

18 JULY 1676

An attachment for 4080 lbs tobacco had been granted to Jonathan Owen against the estate of Tho. Jones. The sheriff had returned 2535 lbs tobacco served in the hands of Jno. Tarr. Owen made his debt appear by a bond dated 14 July 1675. Execution was to proceed with Jones paying court costs. (p. 14)

Maj. West and Mr. Bally exited the court; Mr. Johnson entered. (p. 14)

Tho. Bell entered a suit for 909 lbs tobacco against Danl. Boiles, who failed to appear. Ordered that judgment and court costs pass against the sheriff if Boiles did not appear at the next court. (p. 14)

Mr. Brown exited the court; Capt. Littleton and Capt. Custis entered. (p. 14)

Wm. Freeman (attorney: Mr. White) sued Elizbeth Robinson, but the court, finding no cause for action, dismissed the suit with Freeman paying court costs.
Because there was no cause for action in Wm. Freeman's suit against Eliz. Robinson, she petitioned for a nonsuit, which was granted with Freeman paying court costs. (p. 14)

Capt. Custis exited the court for the following action:
Elizabeth Stratton sued Wm. Morgan (attorney: Mr. Tankard) for defamation, but the court found no cause for action and dismissed the suit.
On the petition of Wm. Morgan, a nonsuit was granted against Elizabeth Stratton, who was also to pay court costs. (p. 14)

Capt. Littleton exited the court for the following action:
Mr. Jno. Hanson made it appear that Mr. Thomas Teakle owed him 3456 lbs tobacco. Ordered that Teakle immediately give Hanson a bill for payment of the debt on 10 October and pay court costs. (p. 14)

Mr. Jno. Mikell, Sr., sued Capt. Danl. Jenifer for a debt, but the court dismissed the suit. The case was examined in open court by Southy Littleton, Rich. Bally, Rich. Hill and Jno. Wallop. (p. 14)

Accomack County Court--19 July 1676

Present: Capt. Southy Littleton Mr. Richard Bally
Capt. Rich. Hill Mr. Jno. Wallop (p. 14)

Mr. Wm. Anderson was the foreman for the jury summoned for this court:
Mr. Blacklock   Mr. Wm. Major   Mr. Tobias Selvy
Mr. Tho Barret   Mr. Tho. Morgan   Mr. Jno. Smally
Mr. Jno. Cropier   Mr. Jno. Parks   Mr. Abraham Tayler
Mr. Wm. Fletcher   Mr. Jno. Savage   (p. 14)

In June of 1673, an order had been passed desiring Col. Jno. Custis, Col. Wm. Kendall, Mr. Hugh Yeo and Mr. Edwd. Revel to appraise the estate of Mr. Devorax Browne (deceased). Because they had not done it, Mrs. Tabitha Brown petitioned that the court appoint appraisers. The sheriff was ordered to summon Mr. Hugh Yeo, Mr. Edwd. Revell, Mr. Robt. Huchinson and Mr. Wm. Anderson to appraise the estate and bring their appraisal to court by November at the latest. (p. 15)

Jno. Peirce complained that several horses broke into his corn field; he requested that the court appoint two persons to view the damage. Ordered that Mr. Edward Revell and Jno. Fenn view the damaged fence and make a report at the next court. (p. 15)

Robt. Custis (attorney: Alex. Swan) sued Jno. Parsons for a debt. The court ordered that it be referred to a jury. It was the jury's verdict that the letter of attorney was not proved. Signed, Robt. Huchinson, foreman.
The court dismissed the suit, and at the petition of Jno. Parsons, ordered that a nonsuit be granted against Robt. Custis, who was also to pay court costs. (p. 15)

The suit of Mr. Jno. Hanson (attorney: Mr. White) against Tho. Jones (attorney: Ch. Holden) was referred to a jury which examined all the evidence; the verdict was that Hanson had no cause for action. Signed, Robt. Huchinson, foreman.
The court dismissed the suit with Hanson paying court costs. (p. 15)

Deposition of James Hill aged about 25 years: On Monday 3 January 1675/76, Hill, along with Jno. Hanson, Amos Bonvill and Tho. Jones was coming into Nanduy Creek in Jno. Hanson's sloop. The creek, being "very much frozen, the sloop remained fast and unmovable in the ice over against or near a tobacco house, which I suppose belonged to Jno. Lecatt." The anchor had been left at the creek mouth "by extremity of weather." Jno. Hanson called Amos Bonvill to go to shore; he said he would get a killick[1] made and send it on board, at which time Tho. Jones was to "fit it and bind thereto a coil of new rope" that they had in the sloop. Two days later, after Jno. Lecat brought the killick, the wind blew very hard and opened the ice, and the sloop began to move. "Tho. Jones made some sail and ran the sloop on ground upon Jno. Lecatt's shore, not having fastened the coil of rope to the killick as Jno. Hanson ordered, but forthwith went on shore to Capt. Littleton's house." There were various chests and casks of goods on the sloop. "I asked if I should take Jno. Hanson's hat with me. The said Tho. Jones replied, 'Let him be damned,' or after the same reviling language, and immediately came on shore." Sworn before Jno. Wise on 26 June 1676, and signed by James Hill. (p. 15)

Jno. Betts summoned Maj. West to court and petitioned for his freedom, but since he did not prove his case, the suit was dismissed with Betts paying court costs. (p. 15)

The suit of Jno. Coale against Andrew Cornelius for a debt was referred to the next court. (p. 16)

Mr. Jno. Hanson started a suit against Tho. Jones, but there appeared to be no cause for action; Jones was granted a nonsuit against Hanson, who was also to pay court costs. (p. 16)

Jno. Lawes' suit against Henry Chancy was dismissed, the court finding no cause for action. (p. 16)

Mr. Robt. Huchinson's suit against Maj. Jno. West over a debt was referred to the next court. West promised to answer the charges against him so a full determination could be made. (p. 16)

Capt. Littleton exited the court for the following two actions:
At the last court an order had been passed against Jno. Cole at the suit of Capt. Southy Littleton as an assignee of Mr. Wm. Sherrwood; Cole became bail for the appearance of Mr. Wm. Whittington. Since Whittington did not appear, it was ordered that the former order be confirmed and that Cole pay the debt of 800 lbs tobacco on 10 October. (p. 16)

---

[1] *A killick was a small anchor often made of a stone enclosed by pieces of wood.*

Jno. Lawes sued Henry Chancy, but there appeared to be no cause for action. A nonsuit was granted against Lawes, who was also to pay court costs. (p. 16)

Information was given to the court that Jno. Watts, cooper, and Jno. Hanning had spoken words derogatory to the Governor's honor. Ordered that the sheriff take them into custody till they posted bond for their appearance to answer charges at the next court. (p. 16)

The suit of Maj. Jno. West against Henry Read (attorney: Charles Holden) for defamation was referred to a jury.
Deposition of James Ewell aged about 35 years, sworn in open court 19 July 1676: About a month ago Ewell met Henry Reade at the house of Jno. Coale and among other things, they discussed the news about the burgesses and that Capt. Littleton was to go. "Read did say that churches were cried down, and if Major West should go burgess, the church would certainly go forward, for he heard that Griff. Savage was to bear half Maj. West's charges over the bay." Signed by Jams. (I) Ewell before Jno. Washbourne.
Deposition of Ann Ewell aged about 30 years, sworn in open court 19 July 1676: Ann swore that her husband James Ewell had declared the truth. Signed by An (E) Ewell before Jno. Washbourne.
Deposition of Tho. Webb aged about 30 years, sworn in open court 19 July 1676: About a month ago Webb was at Jno. Coale's house where Henry Reade was discoursing about the burgesses to several persons, but Webb did not remember who they were. "I heard [Reade] say that Major West might be now, he could not tell, but formerly he was as very a rook as any in the country." Signed by Tho. (X) Webb before Jno. Washbourne.
Deposition of George Russell aged about 24 years, sworn in open court: About a month ago at the house of Jno. Coale, Henry Read said, "People might say what they would, but Maj. West, as he heard, had been as great a rook as any in the county, and for ought he knew, might be still." Signed on 19 July 1676, by George (X) Russell before Jno. Washbourne.
The jury examined the evidence and decided that West was "damnified to the value of ten lbs tobacco." Signed, Wm. Anderson, foreman.
Henry Reade (attorney: Ch. Holden) requested liberty to appeal to the next general court, which was granted. (p. 16, 17)

Jno. Cole sued Saml. Tayler for 441 lbs tobacco; Tayler failed to appear and it was ordered that the sheriff pay the debt if Tayler did not appear at the next court. The case was examined in open court by S. Littleton, Rich. Hill, Rich. Bally and Jno. Wallop. (p. 17)

Hillary Stringer swore in open court that Katherin Bayly, now servant to George Brickhous, had a seven year indenture between herself and George Priest. She had come from Bristoll to Virginia on the ship *Wm. & John* in 1675, which was when her term of service was to begin. Signed 17 July 1676, by Hillary Stringer before Jno. Washbourne. (p. 17)

Wm. Nock gave notice that a wild black ox was keeping his cattle from entering his pen. If he owner did not claim the ox, it was Nock's intention to kill it; he would pay the rightful owner when he appeared. Signed, Wm. Nock. Recorded 14 August 1676. (p. 18)

A certificate (recorded 14 August 1676) was granted to Capt. Danl. Jenifer for 650 acres for transporting:

George Archebold	George Floard	Jno. Wafers
Jno. Barker	Henry Gibbons	Edward Williams
Jno. Bellmame	Edward Huges	Rich. Williams
Wm. Blomefeild	Dorothy Oliver	(p. 18)
Jane Dyton	Saml. Pomeray	

Tabitha Brown, administrator of her deceased husband's estate, reminded the court that they had appointed appraisers who had neglected to appraise her husband's estate. She petitioned that the court order them to do the task or order others to do it. Recorded 14 August 1676. (p. 18)

Accomack County Court--18 December 1676

Present: Capt. Southy Littleton   Capt. Edm. Scarburgh
Maj. Jno. West   Mr. Richard Bally (p. 19)

Jno. Cole petitioned to be administrator of the estate of Jno. Flack (deceased), who owed Cole 7000 lbs tobacco. Ordered that Cole post security and take Flack's estate into his custody until letters of administration could be legally granted. (p. 19)

The suit of Jno. Coale against Wm. Smith for a debt was referred to the next court at Smith's request. (p. 19)

Capt. Custis entered and Capt. Littleton exited the court. (p. 19)

Capt. Southy Littleton's servant boy named Wm. Hall was judged to be 17 years old and was ordered to serve accordingly. (p. 19)

Capt. Littleton entered the court. (p. 19)

Jno. Thomson's servant girl named Mary Dobins was judged to be 15 years old and was ordered to serve accordingly. (p. 19)

Capt. Littleton exited the court for the following action:
Capt. Littleton's servant boy named Thoms. Rolph was judged to be 14 years old and was ordered to serve accordingly. (p. 19)

The suit of Wm. Arriskin, attorney for Edwd. Palmer, against Tho. Jones was dismissed; no one appeared to prosecute. (p. 19)

"Upon the petition of Maj. Edmd. Bowman denying letters of administration upon the estate of Jno. Hogben, deceased," it was ordered that Bowman take possession of Hogben's estate and be answerable until letters of administration could be legally granted. (p. 19)

Tho. Jones sued Mr. Jno. Hanson but did not appear to prosecute. At the petition of Arthur Robins (attorney for Hanson) a nonsuit was granted against Jones, who was also to pay court costs. (p. 19)

Mr. Jno. Hanson sued Capt. Wm. Gingee over a debt but did not prove his bill. Ordered that the suit be dismissed. (p. 20)

Mr. Wm. Anderson, attorney for Mr. Tho. Welburne, sued Richard Bundick, Sr., for 1228 lbs tobacco, but Bundick failed to appear. If he failed to appear at the next court, the sheriff was to be responsible for the debt. (p. 20)

Accomack County Court--19 December 1676

Present: Capt. Southy Littleton   Mr. Tho. Browne
Capt. Wm. Custis   Capt. Edm. Scarburgh (p. 20)

Rowland Savage's servant boy named Thomas Nucomes was judged to be 16 years old and was ordered to serve accordingly. (p. 20)

19 DECEMBER 1676

The will of Henry Truitt was probated by the oaths of Robert Burton and Wm. Lewis. (p. 20)

Jno. Truit petitioned to select his guardian; his choice, Robert Burton, was ordered to "take the said Truit into his tuition and care." At the next court he was to give an account of the orphan's estate. (p. 20)

David Gibbon admitted owing 400 lbs tobacco to Mr. Jno. Hanson. He was to pay the debt and court costs. (p. 20)

Deposition of Richard Jones, Sr., aged about 26 years: Jones positively declared that Wm. Simons struck Jones, who was Capt. Edmd. Scarburgh's overseer at the time.

Attestation of Jane Gin aged about 25 years: She and many others had often heard Wm. Simons brag that he would strike Richard Jones "let him be an overseer or a devil." Jones "finding occasion" struck Simons, who then "rose up and furiously assaulted the said Jones." They fought for about an hour; finally, Jones "overmastered [Simons] and beat him." Simons said he had resolved to try to beat Jones, "for to tell the truth, I thought I could beat you, but you are too hard for me." Signed 17 December 1676, by Jane (/\) Gin. Witness: Tho. Hedges.

Deposition of James Steavens aged about 26 years: At different times he had heard Wm. Symons swear that he would strike Richard Jones "let him be an overseer or devil, and that he did his best endeavor to beat him." Steavens said, "Well, you are a fool to tell everyone your mind so much and brag how you have beaten Richard Jones and Tho. Willson. You will bring an old house upon your head." Sworn before Richard Bally on 18 December 1676. Signed, James (C) Stevans.

It appeared to the court by the oath of Richard Jones, Sr., and other circumstances that Wm. Simons, while servant to Capt. Edm. Scarburgh, struck Richard Jones, Sr., his overseer. Ordered that Simons serve his master an additional year as mandated by the law and pay court costs. (p. 20, 21)

Capt. Custis exited the court and Capt. Edmd. Scarburgh entered. (p. 21)

Richard Bundick admitted owing 1228 lbs tobacco to Thomas Welburne. Bundick was ordered to pay the debt and court costs; the former order against the sheriff was reversed. (p. 21)

Jno. Barnet, Jr., entered an action against Jno. Harris but filed no petition. A nonsuit was granted against Barnet, who also was to pay court costs. (p. 22)

Nicholas Tubbins sued Jno. Scamell for defamation, but the court dismissed the suit with Tubbins paying court costs. (p. 22)

Richard Bundick, Sr., on behalf of the administrators of Col. Edmd. Scarburgh, confessed a judgment of 4000 lbs tobacco and court costs to be paid to Maj. Jno. West. (p. 22)

Nicholas Tubbins sued Jno. Scamel, but their appeared to be no cause for action; upon the petition of Scamel, a nonsuit was granted against Tubbins, who was also to pay court costs. (p. 22)

Mr. Tho. Welburne sued Jno. Coale for a debt; Coale's attorney requested and was granted that the case be referred to the next court "he being at that time in the public service." (p. 22)

Upon the petition of Mr. Tho. Welburne, a caveat for 1300 lbs tobacco was entered against the estate of Jno. Flack, deceased. (p. 22)

Upon the petition of Maj. Jno. West, a caveat for 600 lbs tobacco was entered against the estate of Jno. Flack, deceased. (p. 22)

Ordered that the sheriff take into custody the estate of Nicholas Rogers, deceased, sell it at an auction and provide an account to the court; the estate was so small that no one would administer it. (p. 22)

Wm. Chace made it appear to the court that Nicholas Rogers' estate owed him 604 lbs tobacco; ordered that the estate pay the debt and court costs. (p. 22)

The Governor commissioned Capt. Southy Littleton, gentleman, "to collect and secure all castle duties in the county." All former commissions were voided. Signed 6 December 1676, William Berkeley. Recorded 26 February 1676/77, by Jno. Washbourne, Accomack County court clerk. (p. 23)

Deposition of Jane Diton aged about 27 years: Said that Jno. Hogben gave Mrs. Bowman the bill of Capt. Jenifer, "if she pleased to accept of it, and he hoped that Capt. Jenifer would pay it without any trouble." Hogben gave a horse "to Mr. Boyle if [Hogben] did not come home again." Hogben said that Maj. Bowman owed him some tobacco which he wanted to pay a debt to Jno. Coale; anything left after paying that debt he gave to Maj. Bowman. Sworn in open court 18 December 1676, Jane (X) Dyton. (p. 23)

Perry Leatherbery aged about 12 years said the same as Jane Dyton. Sworn in open court 18 December 1676, before Jno. Washbourne. (p. 23)

Jno. West swore that Mr. Huchinson owed West no more than 442 lbs tobacco. Signed 18 December 1676, Jno. West. (p. 23)

Ordered that the court be adjourned till 16 January. Signed, Southy Littleton, Wm. Custis, Tho. Browne, Edmd. Scarburgh and Richard Bally. (p. 23)

Accomack County Court--2 February 1676/77

Present: Col. Southy Littleton   Mr. Richard Bally
           Capt. Edmd. Scarburgh   Mr. Obedience Johnson (p. 24)

Mr. George Nikolas Hack was foreman of the jury summoned for this court:

Rich. Cutler	Wm. Martiall	Wm. Stevans
Jno. Fenn	Bartholemew Meares	Jno. Stratton
Tho. Fookes	Henry Reade	Hendrick Waggaman
Wm. Freeman	Jno. Savage	(p. 24)

Phillip Fisher's servant boy named Jno. Dowman was judged to be 18 years old and was ordered to serve accordingly. (p. 24)

Issaack Dix's servant boy named Thomas Pope was judged to be 13 years old and was ordered to serve accordingly. (p. 24)

Because Capt. Daniel Jenifer, a former commissioner, had proved to be a loyal subject, "always ready to serve and obey me, his Majesty's Governor, in suppressing the present rebellion," he was again appointed commisioner. Signed 8 December 1676, William Berkeley.
Capt. Danl. Jenifer was received and sworn as a commissioner for Accomack County as commanded by the Governor. (p. 24)

Wm. Freeman sued Jno. Betts and his wife, but in the exhibited bill, he did not complain of anything against them. Ordered that the suit be dismissed with Freeman paying court costs. (p. 24)

Samuel Tayler was granted an attachment of 1600 lbs tobacco against the estate of Thomas Boise. Tayler supposed the tobacco to be in the possession of Capt. Danl. Jenifer, who promised to give an account at the next court. Ordered that the case be referred to the next court and that Tayler be granted precedence against the estate of Boise. (p. 25)

Capt. Danl. Jenifer entered the court. (p. 25)

Sarah Painter, wife of Richard Painter, complained that while her husband was absent from the county on business his creditors procured attachment against Painter's estate and goods, including the clothes belonging to Sarah and her children. The court "considered her condition" and ordered that she have her bedding and necessary apparel for herself and her children. (p. 25)

Mr. Riding entered the court. (p. 25)

Jno. Coale made it appear that Wm. Smith owed him 4200 lbs tobacco. Ordered that Smith pay the debt and court costs.
Smith requested to appeal to the next general court; it was granted after security was posted according to law. (p. 25)

Jno. Midleton petitioned against Mrs. Tabitha Brown (attorney: Mr. Tankard) for his freedom corn and clothes; he requested a jury, which was granted.
By the testimony of Capt. Wm. Gingee and Ann Whyt, the jury was convinced that Jno. Midleton was free. Signed 2 February 1767/77, George Nich Hacks.
The jury's verdict was confirmed, and it was ordered that Midleton be free; Mrs. Browne was to pay corn and clothes according to the custom of the country along with court costs. Signed, Southy Littleton, Tho. Ryding, Edmd. Scarburgh, Obedience Johnson, and Rich. Bally. (p. 25)

Accomack County Court--3 February 1676/77

Present: Col. Southy Littleton   Capt. Edm. Scarburgh
           Capt. Danl. Jenifer   Mr. Obedience Johnson
           Capt. Wm. Custis   Mr. Jno. Wallop (p. 26)

Because Wm. Bedar (who had not proved his petition) and Mr. Tho. Brown "consented to join issue concerning wages", the suit was dismissed. (p. 26)

Mr. Brown entered the court; Capt. Custis exited the court. (p. 26)

Edward Hamond petitioned the court concerning a boat he had found; ordered that he give security and keep the boat in his possession. He was to pay 50 lbs tobacco each to Wm. Trafford and Nathanl. Bradford and pay what Capt. Custis would charge for the trouble of securing the boat. Hamond was to keep the boat in safety till the rightful owner appeared. (p. 26)

Capt. Custis and Mr. Riding entered the court. (p. 26)

Ordered that Nicholas Millechop take into his custody the estate of Henry Armstrong (deceased) and bring an account of it to the next court. He was to make "diligent inquiry" to see if anything had been embezzled or taken away. (p. 26)

Capt. Edm. Scarburgh exited the court for the following action:
At the petition of Mr. Wm. Anderson, attorney of Mr. Tho. Welburne, it was ordered that a caveat for 500 lbs tobacco be entered against the estate of Henry Armstrong (deceased). (p. 26)

Nicholas Millechop claimed that Tho. Gill's estate owed him 3300 lbs tobacco. Ordered that Millechop take Gill's estate into his custody (after giving security) and give an account at the next court. Examined and signed by Sou. Littleton and Ed. Scarburgh. (p. 26)

Mr. Bally entered the court; Col. Littleton, Mr. Wallop and Capt. Jenifer exited the court. (p. 26)

Ordered that the suit of Mr. Robt. Huchinson against Maj. Jno. West over a debt be referred to a jury; the sheriff was to impanel a jury capable of accounting so they could audit the records and bring their report to the court. Their verdict would be the final determination of the case. Signed, Wm. Custis. (p. 26)

Petition from Jone Ocahone, widow of Phillip Ocahone of Accomack County, to Sir Wm. Berkeley, Governor of Virginia: Phillip had married Jone when she was a widow with a "good, reasonable estate left by her former husband of Watts Island in the aforesaid county by name Walter Tayler." In his lifetime, Phillip Ocahone completely wasted and consumed the estate and ran himself far into debt, to the utter ruin of Jone and her poor children. "Phillip, for his felonious and rebellious actions, having justly suffered death", Jone complained that she was

being unjustly prosecuted and sued by the creditors of Phillip. Jone implored the governor to grant clemency and command all persons to desist from suing her for any debts contracted by Phillip Occahone, her late husband.
The above petition was granted; the Governor forbade all persons from suing Jone Ocahone for any debt contracted in the lifetime of Phillip Ocahone. Signed 11 January 1676/77, Wm. Berkeley.
In addition, at the signing of the above, the Governor declared that Jone Ocahone should enjoy the estate in her possession. Testified and signed by Daniel Jenifer. Recorded 14 March 1676/77, by Jno. Washbourne. (p. 27)

Deposition of Wm. and Rebecca Benston aged 34 and 39: On 22 May 1676, German Gillet, Wm. Smith and Jno. Coale came to the Benston house to "assign over" a bond of Phill. Occahone's from Wm. Smith to Jno. Coale, who accepted the bond as pay, provided Smith made the bond appear to be due. Smith demanded a [signature] to prevent further trouble, and Coale answered that "time was short and he had a great way home." Coale requested the Benstons to witness the agreement and passed an obligation to Smith which was in balance of all accounts between them payable in the hands of Occahone. When Smith expressed unwillingness, Coale retorted that he "might very well accept of a hogshead of tobacco in Occahone's hands"; he had gotten that great a sum from the paymaster's hands. Signed by Wm. Benston in open court 3 February 1676/77.
"We very well remember that Jno. Coale accepted it as his own both before and after signing." Signed by Rebeca (R) Benston in open court 3 February 1676/77. (p. 28)

Wm. Morgan addressed the "Worshipful Honorable Gentlemen" of Accomack County and confessed that he had done Jno. Stratton a "great deal of wrong in abusing of him in his absence" by saying that he had killed a calf. Admitting that he had never known Stratton to wrong any man, Morgan regretted the injuries he had caused and said, "I am very sorry for it and will never do the like again." Signed, Wm. (0) Morgan.
After Wm. Morgan acknowledged his abuse of Mr. Jno. Stratton in open court, Stratton acquitted him of the same. (p. 28)

Capt. Wm. Custis, a justice of the peace and coroner, impaneled a jury to investigate the death of Mr. Mathew Scarbrow's servant named Jno. Stephenson, who was found dead 26 January 1676/77, in a chamber at the house of Capt. Danl. Jenifer at Gargaphia. The jury's verdict was that Stephenson had caused his own death by hanging himself by the neck with a piece of red cloth edging fastened to one of the chamber window bars. Signed 27 January 1676/77, by the foreman, Wm. Whittington, and the other members of the jury:

Jno. Bagwell	Samuel Bland	Nicholas Numan
Tho. Bagwell	James Collison	Edward Smith
Jno. Barker	Henry Gibbons	Wm. Smith
Jno. Bellman	Ralph Justice	(p. 29)

Accomack County Court--5 February 1676/77

Present: Col. Southy Littleton   Capt. Richard Hill
           Capt. Wm. Custis   Mr. Richard Bally
           Mr. Tho. Riding   Mr. Jno. Wallop
           Mr. Tho. Browne   Mr. Obedience Jnoson (p. 29)

Richard Jones confessed a judgement of 2612 lbs tobacco due to Jno. Cole. Signed 5 February 1676/77, Richard Jones, Sr. Witnesses: Edward Dolby and Ann (X) White. Sworn in open court by Edw. Dolby.

Mr. Jno. Tankard, attorney of Richard Jones, Sr., admitted the above debt, which was to be paid with court costs. (p. 29)

Tho. Tyra confessed a judgment of 320 lbs tobacco due to Henry Read. The debt was to be paid with court costs. (p. 30)

By the oath of Mr. George Nich. Hack, it appeared to the court that the estate of Nich. Rogers (deceased) owed Mrs. Boate 700 lbs tobacco. Ordered that the estate pay the debt and court costs. (p. 30)

Tho. Hall petitioned against Richard Price for a debt of 2344 lbs tobacco for goods received. Ordered that Price pay 1000 lbs tobacco, make satisfaction to his master for a 30 day absence, and pay all costs of the suit. Since Richard White, another of Hall's servants, had run away with Price, it was ordered that White pay the other part of the debt when he was captured. (p. 30)

Capt. Littleton exited the court. (p. 30)

Col. Southy Littleton had subpoenaed Mr. Roger Mikell as a witness, but Mikell refused to swear. Ordered that he be committed to the sheriff's custody and remain there till he gave evidence upon oath. (p. 30)

Accomack County Court--6 February 1676/77

Present: Col. Southy Littleton   Mr. Richard Bally
                Capt. Daniel Jenifer   Mr. Obedience Johnson
                Capt. Wm. Custis   Mr. Jno. Wallop (p. 30)

Deposition of Simon Thomas aged about 40 years, 6 February 1676/77: About 6 August, Thomas heard Thomas Bushall promise Dr. Winter 600 lbs tobacco, 3 pounds sterling or the value in goods on the condition that Winter would take Bushall into his care. Winter replied that there were no nurses, but if he could get a convenient place and a good nurse, he would consider it. After that, Bushall procured a place at Robt. Huit's, where Dr. Winter cared for him till he was well. After Bushall's recovery, Thomas met him at Huit's house and asked him how Dr. Winter did. Bushall "bade me tell him that he is a son of a whore, and I replied, 'You may do the message yourself.'" Signed, Symon (|) Thomas.

Andrew Winter was granted a judgment of 793 lbs tobacco and court costs against Tho. Bushell, who had the liberty of paying in goods or money. (p. 30, 31)

The suit of Mr. Robt. Huchinson against Maj. Jno. West was to go to a jury, but by mutual consent the difference was put to arbitration. The jury was discharged. (p. 31)

Accomack County Court--7 February 1676/77

Present: Capt. Southy Littleton
            Capt. Daniel Jenifer   Capt. Rich. Hill
                 Capt. Wm. Custis (p. 31)

Tho. Clifton acknowledged a judgment of 500 lbs tobacco and court costs due to Mr. Edm. Bowman and Griff. Savage on behalf of the parish. (p. 31)

Maj. Jno. West sued Jno. Coale but did not file his petition according to law; ordered that a nonsuit be granted against West, who was also to pay court costs. (p. 31)

Jno. Reeves obtained an order dated 18 July 1676, for his freedom corn and clothes "in case Nathaniel Bradford did not produce an assignment under

Henry Bradford's hand for five years." Bradford failed to do this, so the court ordered that the former order be confirmed. Bradford was to pay 600 lbs tobacco to Reeves for six months of extra service along with the corn and clothes and the cost of the suit. (p. 31)

Abraham Dorton sued Joseph Nuton for 750 lbs tobacco, but Nuton failed to appear. If he did not come to the next court, it was ordered that the sheriff pay the debt. (p. 32)

Jno. Cole made it appear that the estate of Jno. Hogben (deceased) owed him 2568 lbs tobacco. The debt and court costs were to be paid. (p. 32)

Ordered that the court be adjourned till 16 March. (p. 32)

List of Accomack County tithables for 1676:

Name	Count	Name	Count
Jno. Cropper	4	Jno. Lenham	1
Mathew Shipp	1	Robt. Huit	5
Japhet Cooke	1	David Gibbons	1
Mr. Tho. Teakle	9	Wm. White	1
Tho. Bushall	1	Rich. Niblet	1
Joseph Ames	1	Jno. Lecatt	3
Owen Collenon	5	Wm. Dyne	1
Danl. Darby	1	Samuel Serjeant	1
Wm. Fletcher	3	Tho. Hall	3
Tobias Selvy	1	Wm. Major	3
Jno. Smally	1	Jno. Harris	2
Jno. Marainer	1	Arthr. Robins	5
Mr. Richard Bally	6	Jno. Kellum	1
Abraham Tayler	1	Max. Gore	1
George Charnock	2	James Longo	1
Jno. Rust	1	Col. So. Littleton	11
Morgan Thomas	2	Jno. Cole	3
Tho. Tyzar	1	Jno. Nelson	2
Richard Holland	1	Wm. White	3
Edward Martin	1	Rowland Savage	2
Mrs. Fauset	3	Wm. Williams	1
James Atkins	1	Wm. Jones	1
Richard Kellum	6	Wm. Wouldhase	1
Jno. Rowles	1	Henry Selman	2
Robt. Hudson	-	Stephan Whittman	1
Dormt. Sellivant	4	Capt. Edmd. Scarburgh	5
Rich. Hill	1	George Gin	1
Henry Reade	3	Tho. Willson	1

James Steavens	1	Tho. Maddux	2
Edward Bird	1	Jno. Truman	1
Joseph Clarke	1	Tho. Bell, Jr.	4
Tho. Johnson	3	Henry Scot	1
Joseph Pittman	2	Munston Foster	1
Jno. White	1	Wm. Yeo	3
Jno. Barnet	1	Daniel Byles	1
Mrs. Charleton	3	Jno. Burt	2
Roger Kirkman	1	Dennis Sellivant	1
Mr. Robt. Huchinson	7	Tho. Savage	1
Jno. Feild	3	David James	2
Mr. Geo. Nich. Hack	5	Wm. Alby	3
Andrew Cornelison	1	Edmd. Kelly	4
Peter Yorke	1	Jeptha Johnson	2
Hend. Waggaman	2	Lt. Col. Jno. Tillny	6
Mrs. Tab. Browne	16	Georg Brickhouse	5
Francis Roberts	2	Henry Stott	1
Rich. Welch	1	Laurence Atteage	1
Jno. Parks	1	Jno. Dolby	2
Alexdr. Addison	3	Giles Cope	2
Jno. Booth	2	Jno. Prettiman, Jr.	1
Jonha (sic) Jackson	3	Nich. Laurence	1
Jno. Savadge	2	Henry Bramble	1
Jno. Smith	4	Wm. Whright	1
Wm. Cobb	2	Saml. Glew	2
Robt. Watson	2	Edmond Joynes	1
Nich. Layler	3	George Smith	1
Jno. Hamering	1	Jno. Thomson	3
Danl. Esham	1	Mr. Obedience Johnson	4
George Duy	2	Jno. Scamell	1
Isaack Jacob	2	Wm. Cutting	1
Ralph Doe	3	Henry Lurton	1
Jno. Sheppard	5	Nich. Tubbin's man	1
Tho. Parrimore	5	Mr. Jno. Mikell	3
Jno. Goreing	2	Jno. Greene	1
Tho. Marshall	1	Edward Dolby	1
Jno. Smith	1	Roger Barker	3
Mr. Tho. Browne	4	Jno. Read	1
Jno. Corr	4	Mr. Tho. Ryding	4
Rich. Sheale	3	Widow Parramore	3
Phill. Fisher	2	Robt. Peale	1
Tho. Gittings	1	Emanel Hall	1
Tho. Barton	1	Redrick Powell	1

7 FEBRUARY 1676/77

Wm. Nock	3	James Bonewell	2
Jno. Willis	1	Stephan Warrington	2
Rich. Holland	2	Teage Andrewes	4
Henry Chancy	2	Robt. Hill	1
Mr. Edward Revell	6	Peter Prichard	2
Richard Franklin	1	Rich. Piwell	2
Jno. Stokely, Sr.	1	Paul Carter	2
Darby Regon	1	Mr. James Matts	7
Henry Williams	2	Mr. James Tuck	1
Wm. Burton	4	Andrew Stott	1
James Walker	1	Jno. Lewis	1
Tho. Bagwell	3	Jon. Watts	1
Danl. Owen	2	Jno. Tayler	3
Jno. Bagwell	3	Jno. Barks	1
Tho. Monford	1	James Fowkes	4
Edmd. Allen	2	Rich. Law	1
Barth. Meeres	4	Jno. Gonsalves	1
Edward Huhin	1	Joseph Nuton	2
Wm. Martiall	1	Richard Painter	2
Peter Parker	2	Tho. Tayler	1
Robt. Watson, Sr.	1	Roger Mikell	4
Nath. Bradford	9	Jno. Wise, Sr.	9
Wm. Parker	1	Jacob Gregory	1
Christopher Sadbury	1	a Negro woman in dispute	1
Isaack Medcalfe	3	Capt. Charles Scarburgh	9
Rich. Garritson	1	Jno. Jones	1
Edward Hamond	5	Edmd. Boman (Onancock)	3
Wm. Traffick	2	Maj. Jno. West	14
Martin Oates	3	Mrs. Mary Scarburgh	2
James Ewell	1	Xophr Calvert son, Charles	1
Wm. Freeman	1	Tho. Webb	1
Owen Daniel	1	Rich. Bundock	3
Amb. White	7	Rich. Bundock, Sr.	2
Edmd. Bowman	10	Robt. Burton	2
Wm. Custis	2	Jno. Tounsen	1
Mr. Wm. Anderson	7	Fran. Wharton	2
Jon. Parker of Mata.	6	Rich Hinman	1
Wm. Silverthorne	1	George Truit	1
Jno. Fenn	2	Wm. Hickman	1
Wm. Willson	1	Henry Truit	1
Rich Cutler	1	Griffin Savage	3
Garet Supple	2	Jno. Abut	1
Jno. Jenkins	5	Wm. Aillworth	1

Robt. Bracy	1	Tho. Black	6
Howel Glading	1	Wm. Jarman	1
Jno. Carter	3	Robt. West	1
Adam Robinson	1	James Trewet	1
Jno. Brocks	4	George Wheeler	1
Edward Carter	4	Edward Breaderton	1
Timothy Coe	3	Mr. Jno. Wallop	8
Roger Miles	1	Samul. Tayler	3
Teage Mickell	1	Xopher Stanly	2
Tho. Smally	1	Jno. Parsons	2
Wm. Norton	1	Jonathen Owen	2
Jno. Evans	1	Jno. Stokely	6
Simond Smith	1	Wm. Kennet	3
Tho. Nubold	4	Jno. Bowen	3
Saml. Crichill	1	Wm. Blake	2
Jno. Parsons	2	Wm. Brightinham	3
Jno. Drumond	1	Tho. Cliffon	2
Saml. Oliver	2	Jno. Francisco, Negro	2
Wonni Macklome	2	Woodman Stokely	2
Roger Bernham	2	Wm. Stokely	1
Arth. Frame	1	Edward Wright	1
George Midleton	1	Wm. Prettiman	1
Tho. Blacklock, Sr.	2	Henry Armestrong	1
Jno. Lawes, Sr.	1	Wm. Benston	1
Jno. Ares	2	Peter Morgan	1
Chr. Thomson	1	Tho. Berret	1
Robt. Davis	1	George West	1
Wm. Browne	1	Wm. Lowen	1
Jno. Marvill	1	Henry Rodgers	1
Peter Clavill	2	Jno. Watts	1
Nath. Dotherty	2	Jno. Renny	3
Jno. Hancok, Jr.	3	Jno. Nellson	1
Jno. Sturges	2	Gueslin Vannetson	2
Rich Johnson, Sr.	2	Capt. Danl. Jenifer	26
Robt. Mason	5	Jno. Bloxum	1
Jno. Cury	1	Wm. Tayler, Sr.	5
Jno. Arue	1	Peter Walker	1
Morris Dennis	2	Evan Davis	1
Dennis Morris	1	Edw. Vahun	1
Josua Smith	1	Nicho. Millechop	3
Finlow Mackwilliams	1	Charles Ratcliff	3
Jno. Onyons	4	Total tithables:	736
Isack Dix	1	(p. 32-34)	

Accomack County Court--16 February 1676/77

Present: Col. So. Littleton   Mr. Rich. Bally
               Capt. Wm. Custis   Mr. Jno. Wallop (p. 34)

Wm. Nock's servant boy named Rich. Nicholes was judged to be 14 years old and was ordered to serve accordingly. (p. 34)

Arth. Robins' servant boy named Jno. Crabtree was judged to be 15 years old and was ordered to serve accordingly. (p. 34)

Frans. Robins' servant boy names Tho. Jeffries was judged to be 17 years old and was ordered to serve accordingly. (p. 34)

Mr. Jno. Wise's servant named Edward Allison was judged to be 18 years old and was ordered to serve accordingly. (p. 34)

The justices and other inhabitants of Accomack County obeyed the King's command to send over all grievances, especially those that had been grounds for the "late troubles and disorders among us being deeply sensible of the late rebellion hatched and acted on the Western Shore by Nath. Bacon, deceased, and accomplices." This had caused great expense and loss of crops because residents had to watch all parts of the shore to hinder the rebels from landing and invading "our coast, where we had received into our protection the bodies of the right honorable Sir Wm. Berkeley and several other good and loyal subjects of His Majesty fled to our parts from the fury and rage of the said Bacon."

1st: "We nor any of us knew any reason for any such rebellion and some or all of us did protest against his actions as rebellious."

2nd: "We humbly desire His Majesty to continue Sir Wm. Berkely Governor in Virginia as long as God shall spare him life."

3rd: Wm. Berkely, upon first coming to Accomack, in consideration of "our readiness to assist him, to the hazard of our lives and fortunes, against the said Rebel Bacon" promised that the Eastern Shore should be free from taxes for 21 years. It was requested that the same be confirmed by His Majesty's royal grant.

4th: Sensible of the "vast charge this unhappy war and rebellion hath put the country to" and expecting it to be defrayed out of the country, "we desire we may be excluded from all and every part of the same, we being no way the cause of it."

Lastly: Informed that the King was about to give the country their quit rents for many years to come, and fearing that the war had now nullified it, "we humbly desire it may still remain good to us, as being no way the cause or knowing of the same. To which we subscribe our hands in open court and pray for his Majesty's, Your Honor's and Governor's health long to continue." Signed, Edmd. Bowman, Robt. Huchinson, Wm. Whittington, Jno. Wise, Tho. Riding, Rich. Hill, Edmd. Scarburgh, Jno. Wallop and Obedience Johnson. Ordered that the clerk make 2 copies of the grievances; one was to be sent as directed and the original was to be put on record and taken to Jno. Coale's house to be sealed before Mr. Tho. Riding. (p. 35)

Accomack County Court--17 April 1677

Present: Capt. Charles Scarburgh   Capt. Richard Hill
Capt. Wm. Custis   Mr. Richard Bally (p. 36)

Richard Hinman's servant boy named Jno. Simpson was judged to be 13 years old and was ordered to serve accordingly. (p. 36)

Mrs. Tabitha Browne's servant boy named Edward Weilding was judged to be 15 years old and was ordered to serve accordingly. (p. 36)

Edmond Kelly's servant boy named Wm. Willson was judged to be 13 years old and was ordered to serve accordingly. (p. 36)

Wm. Willet's servant boy named Lancelot Mukerell was judged to be 13 years old and was ordered to serve accordingly. (p. 36)

Nathaniel Mason, servant to Bartholemew Meeres, presented his indenture and proclaimed that he was willing to serve his master one year beyond the indenture; he desired that it be recorded. (p. 36)

Jno. Parker's servant boy named Wm. Williamson was judged to be 11 years old and was ordered to serve accordingly. (p. 36)

Bridget Morgan was presented for bastard bearing; under oath, she named Edward Jellson as the father. Ordered that the sheriff take Jellson into custody till he gave security for his good behavior and to save the parish from any expenses regarding the child. He was also to pay court costs. (p. 36)

Jno. Savage confessed a judgment of 500 lbs tobacco due to the church wardens on behalf of the parish for the fine of Bridget Morgan. Ordered that Savage pay the fine on 10 October along with the costs of the suit. (p. 37)

Ordered that the sheriff take into his custody the estate of Joseph Limeger wherever it could be found in the county. He was to sell it at auction and give an account of it at the next court. (p. 37)

Nich. Tubbins petitioned to be discharged from the office of constable. Ordered that Jno. Burch replace him in the same precincts, and the oath was administered to him. (p. 37)

Robt. Adkins, Jno. Moore, Frans. Stokely, Nath. Ratclife and James Camell were prosecuted for not turning in their lists of tithables. The court considered that the times were unsettled, so it was ordered that they only pay the taxes and prosecution charges to the sheriff. The county was to have credit for their taxes for the ensuing year. (p. 37)

Ordered that the suit of Maj. Edmd. Bowman against Mrs. Anna Boate be dismissed, Mrs. Boate's attorney "pleading they were not legally arrested." (p. 37)

Capt. Hill exited the court; Mr. Riding and Capt. Jenifer entered. (p. 37)

By order of the Governor, Capt. Hillary Stringer was to be added to the commission of Accomack County. Signed 2 April 1677, William Berkeley. Stringer was sworn 17 April 1677. (p. 37)

Capt. Hillary Stringer entered the court. (p. 38)

James Harrison confessed a judgment of 907 lbs tobacco and court costs due to Mr. Tho. Welburne. (p. 38)

Ordered that the sheriff take into his custody the estate of Henry Armstrong (deceased) wherever it could be found in the county. He was to sell it at auction, give an account of it at the next court, and pay the creditors according to the priority of the debts. (p. 38)

Wm. Anderson's servant girl named Jenet Bern was judged to be 15 years old and was ordered to serve accordingly. (p. 38)

Capt. Charles Scarburgh exited the court. (p. 38)

The will of Rob. Huit (deceased) was probated by the oaths of Mr. Tho. Teakle and Dr. Andrew Winter. It was approved by the court and ordered recorded. (p. 38)

Samuel Tayler (attorney: Mr. Tankard) obtained an attachment for 1600 lbs tobacco against the estate of Tho. Boise. As promised, Capt. Danl. Jenifer gave an account of the estate in his possession, which amounted to 1000 lbs tobacco. Ordered that judgment issue on the 1000 lbs tobacco with court charges. (p. 38)

Evan Davis confessed a judgment of 1460 lbs tobacco and court costs due to Maj. Edm. Bowman. (p. 38)

Abraham Dorton (attorney: Mr. Tankard) was granted a judgment of 479 lbs tobacco against Joseph Newton (attorney: Ch. Holden). The debt was to be paid with court costs. (p. 38)

Nicholas Millechop made it appear that the estate of Henry Armstrong (deceased) owed him 1700 lbs tobacco; ordered that the debt be paid according to priority of the debt. (p. 39)

Letters of administration were granted to Maj. Edmond Bowman upon the estate of his wife, Ellinor Bowman (deceased). (p. 39)

Richard Hill summoned a jury of inquest to investigate the death of a bastard child born to Elizabeth Man, who was "privately delivered thereof contrary to law." The jury found several injuries on the child, so it was ordered that the sheriff take Eliz. Man into custody till the next court, where she was to appear for further questioning. Ordered that Mary Aires, Mary Finlow, An Brown, and Christian Blacklock be summoned to testify.
The jury's verdict concerning a bastard child born to Elizabeth Man, who reported that it was stillborn: the child was injured on the left breast and in the mouth, and since Eliz. Man was delivered privately, they questioned her "for further light", as they did the reputed father, Peter Booty, who was the first person that came into the house. The jury found that their stories varied. Signed 26 March 1677, by:

Mary Aires	Mary Finlow	Eleanor
Christian	Marie Hill	Macklamie
Blacklock	Rebecca Karte	Ann Marshall
Ann Browne	Lucretia Lewis	Ann Ternan
Patience Drumond	Elizabeth Loame	(p. 39)

Accomack County Court--18 April 1677

Present: Capt. Wm. Custis
Capt. Daniel Jenifer   Mr. Jno. Wallop
Mr. Richard Bally   Capt. Hillary Stringer (p. 40)

According to a list signed by Tho. Welburne's attorney, Wm. Anderson, it appeared to the court that Anderson had received several bills, papers and accounts of Jno. Coale (attorney: Mr. Tankard). Ordered that Anderson give credit to Coale for the tobacco received in the list of debts. He was also to return the remaining bills, papers and accounts belonging to Coale in three days. (p. 40)

Maj. Edmd. Bowman made it appear that Wm. Chace owed the estate of Jno. Rogers (deceased) 545 lbs tobacco. As high sheriff, Bowman had been empowered by the court to take the estate into his custody and sell it. Ordered that Chace pay the debt to Bowman along with the costs of the suit. (p. 40)

Tho. Tyra confessed a judgment of 402 lbs tobacco due to Mr. Wm. Anderson. Ordered that he pay the debt and court costs. (p. 40)

Evan Davis made it appear to the court by the oath of Nic. Millechop that the estate of Henry Armstrong (deceased) owed Davis 750 lbs tobacco and a cow and calf. Ordered that the estate pay the debt according to priority and pay court costs. (p. 40)

By an order dated "December the 19th: 79" (sic) [the real date was actually 19 December 1676], the sheriff was ordered to sell at auction the estate of Nich. Rogers (deceased) and present an account to the court. The total of goods and bills due to Rogers amounted to 1859 lbs tobacco; ordered that the sheriff pay the creditors according to priority. (p. 40)

Nicholas Millechop confessed a judgment of 937 lbs tobacco due to Mr. Tho. Welburne. Ordered that he pay the debt and court costs. (p. 41)

Capt. Wm. Gingee owed Mr. Jno. Hanson 2544 lbs tobacco; ordered that Gingee pay the pay the debt and cost of the suit. (p. 41)

Mr. Arthur Upshot, attorney for Wm. Burneside, sued Mr. Wm. Whittington, at whose request the case was referred to the next court. (p. 41)

Mr. Jno. Hanson sued Mr. Wm. Anderson for 20 pounds sterling; Anderson, by his oath, proved payment. Ordered that the suit be dismissed with Hanson paying court costs. (p. 41)

The suit of Mr. Tho. Riding against James Harrison was dismissed, no one appearing to prosecute. (p. 41)

Jno. Parker, attorney of Capt. Wm. Gingee, sued Roger Mikell for 1060 lbs tobacco, but Mikell failed to appear; if he did not appear at the next court, the judgment was to pass against the sheriff. (p. 41)

Robt. Holliday sued Edmd. Allen for 1872 lbs tobacco, but Allen failed to appear. If he failed to appear at the next court, the judgment was to pass against the sheriff. (p. 41)

Mr. Tho. Welburne sued Edward Whright for 1386 lbs tobacco, but the sheriff could not find Whright. Attachment was granted against the estate of Whright wherever it could be found in the county. (p. 42)

Mr. Tho. Welburne sued Jno. Stratton for 775 lbs tobacco, but Stratton failed to appear. If Stratton failed to appear at the next court, the judgment was to pass against the sheriff. (p. 42)

Col. Jno. Stringer sued Tho. Madux but did not prove his petition; ordered that the suit be dismissed. (p. 42)

Mr. Tho. Welburne sued Rich. Jones, Sr., for 534 lbs tobacco, but Jones could not be found by the sheriff. As Jones did not appear to answer the petition, Welburne was granted an attachment against Jones' estate where it could be found in the county. (p. 42)

Mr. Jno. Hanson sued Mr. Wm. Anderson, but the court found no cause for action. A nonsuit was granted against Hanson, who also was to pay court costs. (p. 42)

Col. Jno. Stringer sued Thomas Madux, but the court found no cause for action. A nonsuit was granted against Stringer, who also was to pay court costs. (p. 42)

Mr. George Nich. Hack sued Jno. Parker, as attorney for Capt. Wm. Gingee, for 440 lbs tobacco, but did not prove his petition. Ordered that the suit be dismissed with Hack paying court costs. (p. 42)

Mr. Wm. Anderson, attorney of Capt. Wm. Gingee, was sued by Jno. Coale, who did not prove the debt. A nonsuit was granted against Coale, who was also to pay court costs. (p. 43)

Mr. Wm. Anderson, attorney of Capt. Wm. Gingee, sued Jno. Coale but did not file his petition according to law. A nonsuit was granted against Gingee, who was also to pay court costs. (p. 43)

George Boise was granted a judgment of 340 lbs tobacco against Mr. Robt. Huchinson; it was due for tailor's work done. Ordered that Huchinson pay the debt and court costs. (p. 43)

James Ewell confessed a judgment of 1100 lbs tobacco due to Mr. Welburne. Ordered that Ewell pay the debt and court costs. (p. 43)

Mr. Wm. Anderson, attorney of Capt. Wm. Gingee, sued Armsten Foster for 344 lbs tobacco, but Foster could not be found by the sheriff. Because Foster did not appear to answer the charges, an attachment was granted against his estate where it could be found in the county to pay the debt and court costs. (p. 43)

Ordered that the sheriff summon the grand jury to the next court to give their presentments. Ordered that those delinquent in giving presentments pay the charges incurred by their neglect. (p. 43)

Mr. Geo. Nich. Hack sued Jno. Parker, attorney of Capt. Wm. Gingee, but there appeared to be no cause for action. A nonsuit was granted against Hack, who was also to pay court costs. (p. 43)

Ordered that Jno. Lecat be constable in place of Robt. Huit (deceased); Lecat was to go to the nearest magistrate to be sworn. (p. 43)

Accomack County Court--30 April 1677

Present: Mr. Jno. Wise
Capt. Wm. Custis   Mr. Jno. Wallop
Mr. Richard Bally   Capt. Hillary Stringer (p. 44)

It appeared to the court that Ursula Cumbers agreed with Wm. Chace to serve from 18 April to the last of next October. Ordered that she return to her master's service; at the expiration of the term, Chace was to pay her 450 lbs tobacco. Cumbers was to pay for the court charges. (p. 44)

Robt. Holliday signed a note requesting Mr. Robins to ask the court to reverse the order against the sheriff in the case between Edmd. Allen and Holliday, "for we are at present agreed." Signed, Robt. Holliday.
At the last court an order for 1872 lbs tobacco was passed against the sheriff because Edmd. Allen did not appear to answer the difference between him and Robt. Holliday. Mr. Arthur Robins presented a note signed by Holliday that the difference was settled, and on the petition of Mr. Amb. White, the judgment against the sheriff was reversed. (p. 44)

Joan Reads and Debora Tayler were summoned by Wm. Chace as evidence against Ursula Cumbers. Ordered that Chace pay them for their attendance. Ordered that Ursula pay Chace out of her wages at the expiration of her time of service. She was also to pay court charges. (p. 44)

An act of assembly enjoined magistrates to take an account of the list of tithables in their precincts. Ordered that the inhabitants bring in their lists as follows:
--Mr. Tho. Ryding in Hungar's Parish, as formerly.
--Mr. Obedience Johnson on the south side of Onancock.
--Capt. Edmond Scarburgh from Occahannock to Mr. Revell's Bridge.
--Mr. Jno. Wise from Deep Creek Mill to the north side of Pungoteage.
--Capt. Rich. Hill from Deep Creek Mill to the north side of Pungoteage (sic).
--Mr. Jno. Wallop from Capt. Jenifer's to the line on the Sea Side.
--Capt. Wm. Custis from Capt. Jenifer's to Nathan Bradford's on the Sea Side. (p. 44, 45)

Capt. Custis and Capt. Jenifer exited the court. (p. 45)

The Governor ordered that Capt. Daniel Jenifer be sworn as sheriff for the county. He presented Mr. Jno. Wallop and Mr. Wm. Anderson as security for the due performance of his office. Ordered that the clerk draw up a bond to be sealed and signed at the next court, and ordered that the Governor's order for the appointment and the certificate for Col. Southy Littleton be recorded.
The Governor appointed Capt. Danl. Jenifer to be the high sheriff for the present year. Signed 26 March 1677. Recorded 23 May 1677, by Jno. Washbourne.

Southy Littleton's certificate, written from Nandua, 30 May 1677: At the request of Capt. Danl. Jenifer, Littleton certified that the Governor made him a justice of the peace without making him take the oath of supremacy, and he likewise permitted him to be the high sheriff without taking the same oath. It was therefore Littleton's opinion that only the oath of a sheriff should be administered to him. Signed, Southy Littleton. (p. 45)

Capt. Custis entered the court. (p. 45)

Ordered that the court be adjourned till 18 June. Signed, Jno. Wise, Wm. Custis, Jno. Wallop, Daniel Jenifer, Hillary Stringer and Rich. Bally before Jno. Washbourne. (p. 45)

Wm. Gingee, mariner of London, on 22 June 1674, gave Wm. Anderson power of attorney in the colony of Virginia. Signed, Wm. Gingee. Witnesses: Jno. Parker of Matapany, Jno. Cole. Proved in open court 18 April 1677, by the oaths of Coale and Parker. (p. 46)

Accomack County Court--18 June 1677

Present: Col. Southy Littleton   Capt. Edmond Scarburgh
          Capt. Charles Scarburgh   Mr. Richard Bally
          Mr. Jno. Wise   Mr. Jno. Wallop (p. 46)

Herbert Jeffries, Esquire, [presented] "our honorable Governor's proclamation" prohibiting anyone concerned with the rebellion to bear arms; everyone was required to yield due obedience to the Governor. (p. 46)

Capt. Ch. Scarburgh exited the court. (p. 46)

Joseph Lineger's estate, being one gray mare, was appraised at 1000 lbs tobacco by John Watts and William Lowing and left in the possession of Samuel Tayler, the main creditor. In addition a gun, which was not examined, was in the possession of Peter Walker. Signed, Daniel Jenifer. At the last court the sheriff had been ordered to sell the estate of Joseph Linneger, which was done and an accounting had been given of the mare. Ordered that the mare remain in Samuel Tayler's custody till the next court. Tayler claimed that Linneger's estate owed him 560 lbs tobacco and his taxes for the present year, but Tayler, not having proved his debt, requested till the next court to gather evidence. (p. 46, 47)

At the last court an order was passed against the sheriff at the suit of Mr. Tho. Welburne for the appearance of Jno. Stratton; at this court the sheriff produced Stratton. Ordered that the judgment against the sheriff be reversed. (p. 47)

At the last court an order was passed against the sheriff at the suit of Jno. Parker (attorney for Capt. Wm. Gingee) for the appearance of Roger Mikell; at this court the sheriff produced Mikell. Ordered that the judgment against the sheriff be reversed. (p. 47)

Capt. Phillip Hanger summoned Mr. Obedience Johnson (attorney: Mr. Tankard) to answer a debt of Peter Browne's. Hanger produced a letter of credit signed by Johnson in behalf of Browne; it appeared to the court that the letter was directed to Tho. Cock, and since Hanger had petitioned in his own name, the suit was dismissed with Hanger paying costs. (p. 47)

Maj. Bowman entered and Mr. Bally exited the court. (p. 47)

Tho. Bell (attorney: Mr. Tankard) sued Maj. Edmd. Bowman for 600 lbs tobacco but did not prove the debt. The suit was dismissed with Bell paying court costs. (p. 47)

Maj. Bowman entered the court. (p. 47)

Joseph Nuton petitioned to continue caring for Sarha (sic) Eborne. Ordered that Mary (sic) Eborne continue with Nuton till reaching 18 years of age unless she married. Nuton was to take an account of the estate and present it to the next court. (p. 47)

Maj. Gen. Custis entered the court for the following action:
Capt. Issack Foxcroft was granted a judgment of 5890 lbs tobacco against Jno. Coale. It was to be paid 10 October with court costs. (p. 48)

Capt. Ed. Scarburgh exited the court. (p. 48)

Mary Windham petitioned that her illegitimate son be removed from the care of Mrs. Charleton, who was willing to be discharged; Wm. Fletcher had taken the responsibility of the child. Ordered that Fletcher keep the child in "his tuition and care" until he reached the age of 21 years. Fletcher was to post security to save the parish from expense, pay court charges and have the child christened. (p. 48)

Mr. Robt. Huchinson sued George Boice for assault and battery; the case was referred to the next court. (p. 48)

Mr. Bally entered and Maj. Bowman exited the court. (p. 48)

Maj. Edmond Bowman, as church warden, presented the following for fornication and having a bastard child:
--Elizabeth Peacock, servant to Maj. Edmd. Bowman
--Mary Ballard, servant to Mr. Tho. Teakle
--Margret Hill, servant to Mr. Robt. Huchinson
--Margret Rickman, servant to Mr. Jno. Coale
--Mary Knight, alias Hill, being late married to Jacob Hill
--Rebecca Knight, servant to Mr. Matts
--Margret Reydon
--Scotch Betts, recent servant to Mr. Wallop
--Elizabeth Man, servant to Edward Brotherton
Presented for not registering their children's ages:
--Frans. Roberts
--Mr. Richard Kellum, Sr.
Presented for other offenses:
--Peter Yorke for breaking the Sabbath
--George Johnson and Timothy Coe for "unlawfully assembling themselves amongst other companies as speakers at Quaker meetings"
Ordered that the above persons be summoned to appear at the next court to answer their presentments. (p. 48)

The grand jury requested to be discharged, having served their year; the court dismissed them.
Ordered that the sheriff summon a new grand jury and that they appear at the next court to be sworn. (p. 48, 49)

The estate of Henry Armstrong was appraised by Jno. Watts and Wm. Boum by the order of Daniel Jenifer, the sheriff. Items brought before them were valued at 1840 lbs tobacco and included: a red shag rug, Indian bowls, leather feather pillows, an old hair pillow, a trunk and chest, 7 cattle and a barrel of rotten Indian corn. George West acknowledged owing the estate 890 lbs tobacco, making the total value 2730 lbs tobacco. Signed 5 May 1677, Jno (X) Watts and Wm. (X) Boum.
More of the estate "not brought to light" was affirmed by the neighbors: Griff. Savage had two sows, Capt. Foxcroft had a gun, and Jno. Stokely of Assewoman had, without permission, taken away some red cloth, white linen, some peas and some Indian corn.

Henry Armstrong's estate paid Nicholas Millechop (1469 lbs), Evan Davis (785), Maj. Bowman for taxes and fees (300), the sheriff (136), and the appraisers (40), which equaled 2730 lbs tobacco. Signed, Daniel Jenifer. Recorded 2 July 1677, by Jno. Washbourne. (p. 49)

Robt. Dunbarr petitioned against his master, James Fowkes, for his freedom corn and clothes. Ordered that Dunbarr receive the corn and clothes after serving 12 days for his 6 day absence and repaying the 200 lbs tobacco which Fowkes paid Evan Davis for bringing Dunbarr home, as was certified by Mr. Jno. Wise. (p. 49)

Certificate was granted to Arthur Robins for 800 acres for transporting:

Frans. Barnes	Ann Meares	Susanna Shelle
Jno. Borrick	James Norris	Walter Stevenson
Margret Cooper	Jno. Perofrank	Mary Waterland
Jno. Crabtree	Charles Roberts	Sara Watson
James Heuse	Reuth Rogers	(p. 50)
Elizabeth Howerd	Richard Sanders	

The court records were examined in open court 19 June 1677. Signed by Southy Littleton, Edmond Bowman, Richard Hill, Richd. Bally, Jno. Wallop (alias) and Court Clerk Jno. Washbourne. (p. 50)

Accomack County Court--19 June 1677

Present: Mr. Southy Littleton   Mr. Richard Bally
            Maj. Edm. Bowman   Mr. Jno. Wallop (p. 50)

At the request of Capt. Daniel Jenifer (sheriff), Jno. Bellmaine was sworn as bailiff for the upper part of the county--from Maj. Edm. Bowman's on the Sea Side to and including Chesinessicks on the Bay Side up to the Virginia/Maryland line. (p. 50)

Capt. Hill entered the court. (p. 50)

Jno. Bacon, servant to Jonah Jackson, was brought to court where he produced an indenture in which "he was bound at the Toulsel in Bristol for seven years from the arrival of the *Wm. and Ann*, the ship he came into this country on." Bacon admitted that "he changed his name, by the invasion of the spirit that took him up, to Jno. Smith, by which name he

19 JUNE 1677   43

was persuaded to sign the said indenture." The court judged that Bacon should serve his master seven years, according to the indenture. (p. 50)

Mr. Arthur Upshot, attorney of Wm. Burnesides, (attorney: Ch. Holden) sued Mr. Wm. Whittington (attorney: Mr. Tankard). Whittington pleaded that the debt was not demanded according to act, and Upshot craved an order for immediate pay. Ordered that the suit be dismissed. (p. 50)

Mr. Wm. Whittington entered an action against Wm. Burnsides, who could not be found. Whittington craved an order of attachment against Burnsides' estate; Arthur Upshot appeared to bail the attachment. Ordered that the suit be referred to the next court with Upshot putting up security to make good all damages that might accrue. (p. 51)

At the last court it was ordered that Elizabeth Man be kept in custody till this court to be questioned about a bastard child of which she was privately delivered. The court examined all evidences and found no cause for further detention. (p. 51)

Maj. Jno. West was granted a judgment of 500 lbs tobacco and a new bridle against Thomas Barriff, who was also to pay court costs. (p. 51)

Mathew Shipp sued Mrs. Anna Bote for security for 437 lbs tobacco and interest. Ordered that Mrs. Boat give security for 463 lbs tobacco to be paid 10 October along with court costs. (p. 51)

Maj. Edm. Bowman was granted a judgment of 20,000 lbs tobacco against Mrs. Anna Bote. The sum appeared due by a bond exhibited to the court, so it was ordered that Mrs. Bote pay the debt with court costs.
Mrs. Boat requested to appeal to the next general court, which was granted. (p. 51)

Maj. Edm. Bowman, as sheriff, had been ordered to sell the estate of Nicholas Rogers (deceased) at auction and receive the debts due to the estate. It appeared that Jno. Cole owed the estate 448 lbs tobacco. Ordered that he pay the sum to Bowman along with court costs. (p. 51)

At the petition of Mr. Wm. Anderson, on behalf of Elizabeth Smith (orphan), it was ordered that Jno. Stokely give oath at the next court that a full account of Smith's estate had been given and that the estate had been divided according to the intent of the will. Mary Stokely was to go Mr. Jno. Wallop's to take her oath before the next court. (p. 52)

Jno. Charles, by his oath and other evidence, made it appear that he assisted Henry Reade in tending the wounded men brought from across the Bay to Reade's house. Charles helped grind corn and did other necessary duties from 11 October 1676, to 11 January 1676/77, but had received no payment. Ordered that this be certified to the assembly. (p. 52)

Maj. Wm. Spencer sued Edward Hamond for 734 lbs tobacco; Hamond did not appear to answer. The sheriff brought in Jno. Coale as bail. Ordered that Coale pay the debt if Hamond did not appear at the next court. (p. 52)

Mr. Wm. Anderson, overseer of the estate of Elizabeth Smith (orphan), sued Jno. Stokely, at whose request the case was referred to the next court. (p. 52)

Mr. Jno. Hanson was granted a judgment of 400 lbs tobacco against Jno. Cropier for goods delivered, as appeared by the oath of Wiliam Fletcher. Ordered that Cropier pay the debt and court costs. (p. 52)

Col. Jno. Stringer (attorney: Mr. Tankard) sued Tho. Maddux (attorney: Ch. Holden) for a debt, but because there was no proof, the suit was dismissed with Stringer paying court costs. (p. 52)

Deposition of Henry Reade: Last January Reade heard Geo. Boyes admit that he owed William Stevans 500 lbs tobacco and asked to borrow more, saying he wanted Stevans to medically treat ("salivate") him when he came home. Stevans complained that he did not have a convenient house; Boies said he would bargain [for the use of a house] with Reade, but Reade refused. Several times George Boice said that several surgeons had treated him, but that he had benefitted more from [Stevans] than the rest. Signed 19 June 1677, Henry (HR) Reade.

Declaration of Jone Reade: After Boyes requested Wm. Stevans to "spare him more means", Stevans said he had already spared him more than the mentioned 500 lbs of tobacco. Boyse promised to give 200 lbs more, and Stevans condescended to loan him more. If that amount wouldn't do, Boyse said he would find another way. Signed, Jone (/) Reade.

Wm. Steavens was granted a judgment of 380 lbs tobacco against George Boice (attorney: Mr. Tankard); it was the balance of their accounts. The debt was to be paid with court costs. (p. 53)

Mr. Wm. Anderson, attorney of Jno. Anderson, sued James Guy, at whose request the case was referred to the next court. (p. 53)

19 JUNE 1677

George Boyce sued Wm. Steavens, but there appeared to be no cause for action. Steavens was granted a nonsuit against Boice, who was also to pay court costs. (p. 53)

Wm. Martiall made it appear that he gave Mr. Phill. Hanger a bill of Wm. Collins for 400 lbs tobacco that Hanger was to receive or else return; Hanger had not returned the bill. Ordered that Hanger return the bill by 10 November or pay the tobacco with court costs. (p. 53)

An act of the assembly in March left it to each county court to set prices for inn keepers. Therefore the court "set and appointed Jno. Cole a certain price whereby to buy his liquors":
--Brandy: 80 lbs per gallon
--Spanish Wines: 100 lbs per gallon
--French and Portugal wines: 80 lbs per gallon
--Rum: 60 per gallon
--Any drink with sugar: an additional 10 lbs per gallon. Cole was to add a pound of sugar to the gallon if the customer desired it. (p. 54)

Deposition of George Russell aged about 24 years: One night last April he heard Mrs. Charleton correcting her maid, "it being dark and no light in the room." He heard Mary Windham and Mrs. Charleton "make a great crying out." When Mrs. Charleton called Russell to assist her, he said "he believed she wanted none." The next morning Mrs. Charleton's arm was black and blue; she claimed it was done by her servant during the night. Russell said he had often seen "Mary hold the stick when her mistress was correcting of her so to escape from her." Signed 18 June 1677, George (X) Russell. (p. 54)

A note signed by Jno. Cropper and addressed to Mr. Hanson or anyone else concerned asked that Jno. Jolley be permitted to have tools or other items to the value of 400 lbs tobacco. Cropper would pay the debt the next year. Signed 7 February 1675/76, by Jno. Cropper. Proved by Wm. Fletcher: Mr. Hanson delivered goods according to the note. (p. 54)

Deposition of Alexander Dun aged about 26 years: At the April court Dun heard Mr. Huchinson's servant named James (alias Winsewack) ask George Boice to give him credit for some drink; the Indian said he would give some pipes to Boice, who refused, saying the last ones were rotten. The Indian replied, "If you will let me have no drink, you may kiss my arse." Boice called James an "Indian dog", and James retaliated with "English dog." Boice answered that "if [James] called him English dog, he deserved to [have] his jacket thrashed. The Indian bid the said

Boise touch him if he durst, for if he beat him, he would tell his master, and his master should not pay him one pound of tobacco. The said Boise told the said Indian he did not care a turd for his master, but his master might kiss his arse. The Indian dared the said Boise to strike him; upon that the said Boice fell upon the Indian and beat him and kicked him about the house and pulled him by the hair of his head, so that [Dun] spoke to him to strike the said Boise again, and then they fought a good while." Signed in open court 19 June 1677, Alex. (2) Dunn. (p. 54, 55)

Ordered that the court be adjourned till 16 August 1677. Signed, So. Littleton, Edmond Bowman, Richard Hill and Richard Bally. (p. 55)

Charles Leatherbury, along with his brother Peary, supplicated the court: In his will, their father bequeathed to their mother, Elinor, a considerable part of his estate so she could propagate it in trust for their sons. Their mother did this to the utmost, being "a good woman and indulgent mother." Before her remarriage she alienated her estate from her husband's command, intending it for the use of her children at her death. This could be easily proved by her intent and the honesty and good principles of Charles Pakes, the trustee. Capt. Edm. Bowman, lately the husband of their mother, often complained of a hard bargain in marrying a woman with nothing, and claimed it was a demonstration of pure love. However, upon the death of Elinor, Capt. Bowman took advantage of Charles' sickness and youth; without permission he violently took several items out of the house and off the plantation, an act that law could not protect. Charles pleaded that the court command Bowman to return the estate. This petition of Charls Leatherbury was recorded 3 July 1677, by Jno. Washbourne at the request of Maj. Jno. West. (p. 55, 56)

Accomack County tithables for 1677:

Capt. Wm. Custis' list:

Edward Revell	4	Isaack Medcalfe	1
Jno. Stokely, Sr.	1	Hillary Stringer	1
Wm. Burton	5	Jno. Jones	3
Tho. Morinford	1	Tho. Bagwell	2
Wm. Custis	7	Jno. Terry	1
Wm. Nock	4	Rich. Franklin	1
Jno. Willis	1	Samuel Beech	2
Henry Williams	2	Tabitha Browne	19
James Walker	1	Wm. Traford	2
Jno. Bagwell	3	Nath. Bradford	11
Jno. Bushop	2	Barth. Meares	4
Ed. Allen	1	Tho. Clarke	1
		Rich. Costen	1

19 JUNE 1677

Arth. Gaul	1	Stephan Phillby	1
Mart. Otters	1	Jno. West	15
Chris. Adbury	1	Tho. Webb	1
Ellias Garganis	1	Wm. Anoughton	1
James Uell	1	Walter Tayler	1
Henry Chancy	1	**Maj. Bowman's list:**	
Amb. White	10	Wm. White	3
To. Tayler	1	Rich. Bundick	2
Mr. Jno. Wise's list:		Isaack Dix	2
Jno. Fenn	2	Robt. Mason	5
Tho. Fowkes	2	Edmd. Bowman	12
Teage Anderson	4	Jno. Sturgis	2
Jno. Jenkins, Sr.	4	Rich. Johnson, Sr.	2
Steph. Warren	2	Wm. Martiall	1
James Matts	9	Wm. Parker	1
Wm. Silverthorne	1	Peter Parker	1
Wm. Willson	1	Jno. Hancock	2
Tho. Burrowes	1	Rich. Bundick, Jr.	2
Jno. Parker	8	Jno. Hanning	1
Wm. Anderson	7	**Capt. Hill's list:**	
Jno. Lawes	1	George Midleton	4
Jno. Atkins	1	Jno. Caree	1
Robt. Watson	1	Jno. Aierew	2
Rich. Cutler	1	Peter Clavill	1
Phill. Quinton	1	Jno. Abut	1
Peter Prichard	2	Wm. Browne	1
Garret Supple	1	George West	1
Joseph Nuton	1	Jno. Tounsend	1
Tho. Morris	1	Robt. Burton	1
Paul Carter	1	Paptis Nucomb	2
Charles Leatherbury	4	Jno. Prettiman	3
Jno. Lewis	1	Wm. Aillworth	2
James Fowkes	3	Teage Miskell	1
Roger Mikell	5	Howel Glading	2
Darby Regan	1	Tho. Basent	1
Charles Colvert	2	Jno. Lewis, Sr.	3
Jno. Tayler	1	Jno. Brookes	3
Jno. Gonsolvos	1	Jno. Parsons	3
Andrew Stopp	1	Frans. Wharton	2
Jno. Watts	2	Griff. Savage	2
Robt. Hill	2	Edward Brotherton	2
Jno. Wise	12	Roger Ternon	2
Charles Scarburgh	9	Tho. Ryly	2

Wm. Thorton	1	Jno. Moore	1
Arthur Frame	1	Jno. Watts	2
Wm. Wallis	2	Wm. Stokely	2
Jno. Young	1	Robt. Atkinson	1
Jno. Evan	1	Inquisn. Venetson	2
Jno. Millson	1	Saml. Tayler	3
Jno. Renny	4	James Tayler	1
James Booth	1	Allexdr. Massy	1
Onny Mackelamny	2	Cornutus Bence	1
Christopher Thomson	1	Warrn. Harder	1
Tob. Bull	1	Wm. Brightingham	3
George Truit	2	Wm. Benston	2
Rich. Hinman	2	Tho. Barrit	1
Dennis Morris	1	Wm. Blake	1
Wm. Germame	3	Wm. Kennet	1
Tho. Nixson	3	Tho. Cliffon	1
Jno. Barnes	3	Jno. Francisco	1
Finlow Mackwilliam	1	Hen. Rogers	1
Jno. Marvell	1	Xopr. Stanly	2
Joshua Smith	1	Tho. Nubold	4
George Johnson	4	Edwd. Rahan	1
Xophr. Roberts	2	Petr. Morgin	1
Robt. Duguis	1	Roger Miles	1
Tho. Smalpeece	1	Nich. Millechop	3
Jno. Drumond	3	Evan Davis	2
Richard Hill	6	Rich. Williams	1
Timo. Coe	4	Jno. Barke	1
Mr. Jno. Wallop's list:		**Capt. Ed. Scarburgh's list:**	
Jno. Wallop	11	Owen Collonen	6
Danl. Jenifer	24	Jno. Walthom	3
Wood. Stokely	4	Dormt. Sullivant	3
Nath. Ratcliff	2	Rich. Holland	1
Rich. Hasting	1	Morgin Thomas	3
Jno. Stratton	1	Jno. Macome	1
Jno. Stokely	2	Richard Niblet	2
Petr. Watson	1	Tom Symmons	1
Tho. Osburne	4	Joseph Clarke	1
Petr. Walker	1	Wm. Dine	1
Jno. Tarr	1	Michol Huit	6
Wm. Tayler, Sr.	9	Tho. Hedges	1
Jnothn. Owen	2	Edwd. Hichin	1
Jno. Bowen	4	Richard Hill	1
Max. Gore	3	Clemt. Onely	1

19 JUNE 1677

Wm. Wouldhave	1	Henry Reade	3
David Gibbons	1	Roger Kirkman	1
George Charnock	1	Hugh Yeo	6
Jno. Goodman	1	Jno. Frenchman	1
Jno. Holden	1	Danl. Ograyhan	1
Row. Savage	3	**Mr. Tho. Ryding's list:**	
Geo. Nick. Hack	5	Tho. Browne	4
Tob. Selvy	2	Rich. Sheale	4
Henry Sellman	1	Phill. Fisher	2
Tho. Barnet	1	Tho. Madux	2
Wm. Chace	3	Tho. Barton	1
Jno. Rowles	1	David James	2
Ann Charleton	3	Danl. Esham	1
Math. Shipp	1	Jno. Devenish	1
Rich. Bally	6	George Bell	1
Tho. Williams	1	Xophr. Madder	1
Mordy. Edwards	1	Jno. Truman	1
Robt. Hudson	1	George Brickhouse	4
Jno. Nellson	1	Henry Stott	1
Danl. Darby	1	Vrmston Foster	1
Nich. Tyler	1	Lau. Ateage	1
Rich. Kellum	5	Wm. Yeo	3
George Ginn	1	Morg. Weines	1
Rhed. Powell	1	Jno. Dolby	1
Tho. Bushell	1	Jno. Mikell, Jr.	4
Edwd. Burd	1	Jno. Green	4
Jno. Millby	1	Dennis Selivant	2
Wm. Major	4	Henry Lurton	1
Saml. Serjeant	1	Eml. Hall	2
Wm. White	1	Wm. Cuttin	1
Jno. Lecat	2	Jno. Scamell	1
Tho. Hall	3	Jno. Johnson	1
Abrah. Tayler	1	Rich. Melton	2
Jno. Barnet	1	George Roe	1
James Longo	1	Rich. Wood	1
Tho. Teagle	8	Edmd. Kelly	4
Jno. Cole	5	Nich. Tubbins	3
Jno. Croppier	5	Morg. Dewells	3
Robt. Huchinson	6	Jeptha Johnson	2
Southy Littleton	11	Jn. Tillny	4
Hend. Waggaman	1	Jno. Core	4
Edmd. Scarburgh	4	Saml. Glue	2
Wm. Stevans	1	Jno. Thomson	3

Danl. Byles	1	Jno. Parkes	1
Thom. Ryding	4	Edmd. Joynes	1
Mary Parrimore	2	Rich. Garrison	1
Tho. Bell, Sr.	4	Arthr. Robins	5
Roger Barker	3	Jno. Smith, Sr.	4
Giles Cope	3	Alexdr. Addison	4
Mr. Obed. Johnson's list:		Jno. Gordin	2
Tho. Parrimore	5	Obed. Johnson	5
Jos. Pittman	2	Simon Foscue	2
James Scamell	1	Fras. Roberts	4
Nich. Layler	2	Tho. Chapwell	2
George Due	2	Ed. Moore, Sr.	2
Saml. Atkinson	1	Wm. Williams	1
Jno. White	1	Rich. Welch	1
Dorothy Jordain	1	Jno. Booth	2
Tho. Johnson	3	Jno. Smith, Jr.	1
Jno. Sheppard	5	Tho. Marshall	1
James Atkinson	1	Robt. Watson, Sr.	4
Jonas Jackson	5	Total:	768
Jno. Savage	1	(p. 56-58)	

Accomack County Court--13 September 1677

Present: Col. Southy Littleton   Mr. Tho. Browne
             Capt. Wm. Custis   Mr. Jno. Wallop (p. 59)

Mr. Jno. Renny was the foreman of the grand jury sworn for the following year:

Mr. Teige Anderson	Mr. Charles Leatherbury	Mr. Denns. Sellivant
Mr. Wm. Blake	Mr. Jno. Millby	Mr. Jno. Stratton
Mr. Tho. Cliffon	Mr. Rich. Niblet	Mr. Morgan Thomas
Mr. Danl. Derby	Mr. Peter Parker	
Mr. Tho. Fowkes	Mr. Wm. Parker	Mr. James Walker
Mr. Edmd. Kelly	Mr. Xophr Stanly	(p. 59)

Mr. Jno. Stratton proved (by the oath of Capt. Nath. Walker) that Walker, by order of the Governor, had commanded Stratton's shallop in the King's service against the late rebels. The boat was lost at Warrwicks Creek Bay. Ordered that this be a certificate [proving the loss] to the next assembly: Some time last September, Nath. Walker while serving the Governor over the bay for the suppression of Bacon's Rebellion, commanded a shallop belonging to Mr. Jno. Stratton. During a storm this boat was "cast away" in Warrwick Bay. Signed 13 September 1677, Nath. Walker. Proved in open court by the oath of Capt. Nathanl. Walker and recorded by Jno. Washbourne. (p. 59)

Capt. Isaak Foxcroft sued Jno. Cole for 11,010 lbs tobacco; on 18 June 1677, judgment for 5890 lbs tobacco was passed. Coale exhibited his bill in chancery against Foxcroft and claimed that a mistake of 1000 lbs tobacco had been made. Ordered that the debt be 4890 lbs tobacco. (p. 59, 60)

Ordered that the sheriff summon Wm. Fawset to personally attend court tomorrow morning (14 September) to prosecute his complaint against Mrs. Rhody Fawset and Jno. Cropper or deny it. (p. 60)

Frans. Roberts had failed to register his children; ordered that he pay a fine of 100 lbs tobacco and court charges. (p. 60)

Ordered that Richard Kellum, Sr., pay a fine of 100 lbs tobacco and court charges for not registering his children. Kellum claimed that he had registered his children in another parish, so the court gave him till the next court to prove it. (p. 60)

Maj. Jno. West petitioned for 12,240 lbs tobacco; upon his oath, he was granted a certificate to the next assembly. (p. 60)

Pawl Carter swore that he served 50 days under Maj. Jno. West; he also spent six weeks seeking and killing beef for the "country's service" under West's command. He was granted a certificate to the next assembly. (p. 60)

Jno. Sturges was granted a certificate to the next assembly for 46 lbs of butter and 42 lbs of cheese which was delivered for the "country's service", as attested by Maj. Jno. West. (p. 60)

Timothy Coe was granted a certificate to the next assembly for 100 lbs tobacco for salting and resalting meat for the use of the country, as attested by Capt. Jenifer. (p. 61)

Mr. Bally entered the court and Mr. Custis exited. (p. 61)

Mr. Jno. Mikell, Jr., sued Rho. Powell but did not file his petition; a nonsuit was granted against Mikell, who also paid court costs. (p. 61)

Canutus Bence confessed a judgment of 500 lbs tobacco and court costs due to Mr. Jno. Somers, who had married Margret, the executrix of Mr. Jno. Milling (deceased). The sum was the balance of accounts due from Jno. Pash. (p. 61)

Jno. Stratton, empowered by Governor Wm. Berkely to procure or impress needed provisions, certified that he had killed a barren cow belonging to Morris Dennis, for which he gave this certificate 15 October 1676. Signed, Jno. Stratton, commissary. On 13 September 1677, Stratton swore to the above certificate in open court.
Ordered that Morris Dennis be granted a certificate to the next assembly for one barren cow which "was pressed for the public service." (p. 61)

Col. Littleton exited the court for the following action:
Upon the petition of Wm. Emont, it was ordered that a certificate be granted to him for 35 days more than the 10 days that Col. Littleton gave an account of to the last assembly. Littleton acknowledged that he had been mistaken when he delivered the account. (p. 61)

Mr. Wm. Anderson, overseer of the estate belonging to the orphan Eliz. Smith, sued Jno. Stokely (attorney: Cha. Holden). Ordered that the suit be dismissed. Examined in open court by Southy Littleton, Jno. Wise, Rich. Bally and Jno. Wallop. (p. 61)

Accomack County Court--14 September 1677

Present: Col. Southy Littleton   Mr. Richard Bally
                 Mr. Jno. Wise   Mr. Jno. Wallop. (p. 62)

The will of Tho. Blacklock (deceased) was probated by the oath of Jno. Drumond on 14 September and by Tho. Barrit on 15 September. (p. 62)

Maj. Wm. Spencer sued Edward Hammond at the last court when Jno. Coale was returned bail for Hamond's appearance. Spencer failed to appear at this court to prosecute, so the suit was dismissed and the order against Jno. Cole was reversed. (p. 62)

14 SEPTEMBER 1677

Mr. Wm. Whittington sued Wm. Burnesides (attorney: Charles Holden) but failed to appear to prosecute, so the suit was dismissed. (p. 62)

Capt. Wm. Gingee was granted a judgment of 20 shillings sterling and 172 lbs tobacco and court costs against Mr. Tho. Nubold. (p. 62)

Alexander Draper sued Jno. Renny, but since neither of them appeared, the suit was dismissed. (p. 62)

At the last court Joseph Nuton had been granted the care of Sara Eborne. At this court Mary Chapwell petitioned for custody, as Sara was the daughter of Mary's former husband, Wm. Eborne. It was only by Mary's consent that Nuton was to care for Sara till Mary would request her. Since Tho. Chapwell and his wife Mary acknowledged themselves willing to take charge of Sara Eborne and maintain her until she reached 18 years (unless she marry) and to teach her to read within two years, it was ordered that Nuton deliver Sara to Mary Chapwell; the order granted to Nuton was reversed. (p. 62)

Tho. Chapwell, who gave security, was granted administration of the estate of Wm. Eborne (deceased). Ordered that Arthur Robins, Jno. Parkes, Jno. Cob and Giles Cope appraise the estate of Eborne that would be presented by Chapwell and give an account to the next court. (p. 63)

Mr. Tho. Welburne entered action for 7 pounds 18 shillings sterling and court costs against George Pattison, who did not appear to answer the charges. Welburne was granted an order of attachment against the estate of Pattison where it could be found in the county. (p. 63)

Wm. Burnesides (attorney: Charles Holden) sued William Whittington for 8036 lbs tobacco, but Whittington did not appear, and the sheriff returned Jno. Cole as security for Whittington's appearance. If Whittington did not appear at the next court, then Cole would be ordered to pay the debt with court costs. (p. 63)

James Rainy's suit against Jno. Rainy was referred to the next court. (p. 63)

Jno. Cole was granted a judgment of 2300 lbs tobacco against Peter Dolby, who was ordered to pay the debt and court costs. (p. 63)

Jno. Cole sued Robt. Watson, Sr., for 1969 lbs tobacco, but Watson failed to appear. Mr. James Tuck, who was returned as security for Watson's appearance at the next court, was ordered to pay the debt and court costs if Watson did not appear. (p. 63, 64)

Peter Dolby confessed a judgment of 488 lbs tobacco due to Maj. William Spencer. The debt was to be paid with court costs. (p. 64)

A certificate to the next assembly was granted to Tho. Barret for 33 days service under Maj. Jno. West in the King's service. (p. 64)

Jno. Cole was granted a certificate to the assembly for 1920 lbs tobacco; he swore to the particulars in open court. (p. 64)

Maj. Jno. West entered the court. (p. 64)

Jno. Cole was granted a judgment of 837 lbs tobacco against Mr. Tho. Hedges; the debt was to be paid with court costs. (p. 64)

Mrs. Ann Charleton was granted a judgment of 530 lbs tobacco against Mr. Thomas Hedges. At Ann's petition, it was ordered that Hedges give security for payment of the debt and court costs on 10 October. (p. 64)

Col. Littleton exited the court for the following action:
Col. Southy Littleton's suit against Jno. Cropier was referred to the next court at Cropier's request. (p. 64)

Col. Kendall's suit against Mr. Mathew Scarburow was, by consent, referred to the next court. (p. 64)

Col. Southy Littleton's suit against Jno. Stratton for defamation was referred to the next court at the request of Stratton and with the consent of Littleton. (p. 64)

Ordered that the sheriff secure in his custody what he had seized of Mrs. Rhodia Fawset's estate until she gave security to make good the estate that Mr. Jno. Fawset (deceased) had willed to his son, Wm. Fauset, when he arrived to age. (p. 64)

Certificate was granted to Col. Southy Littleton for 850 acres for transporting:

Dan. Bacon	Dick (Negro)	Jno. Harmer
Ellioner Bengor	Mary Dobbins	Hen. Parkes
Rich. Cooper	Jno. Dowman	Tho. Rolph
Tho. Davis	Wm. Hall	Mary Savage

14 SEPTEMBER 1677

| Rich. Smith | Richard White | Rich. Woodcraft |
| Trulace (Negro) | Jno. William | (p. 65) |

Col. Littleton entered the court and Maj. West exited. (p. 65)

Certificate was granted to Maj. Jno. West for 250 acres for transporting:
  Roger Dorthion   James Foster   (p. 65)
  Margaret E   Jno. Welchman

Mr. Bally exited the court. (p. 65)

Mr. Richard Bally's suit against Jno. Cropper was referred to the next court. (p. 65)

With John Cropper's consent, it was ordered that he return the two cows (and their increase) that Maj. Edm. Bowman had previously given to his granddaughter Eliz. Cropper. The animals were to be delivered to the donor for the use of the child. (p. 65)

Mr. Bally and Maj. West entered the court. (p. 65)

Wm. Anderson, attorney of Jno. Anderson, entered action against James Guy for 1200 lbs tobacco, but Guy failed to appear. The judgment with court costs was to be granted against the sheriff if Guy did not appear at the next court. (p. 65)

The suit of Charles Parkes against Maj. Edm. Bowman was referred to the next court. (p. 65)

The difference between Mr. Wm. Anderson upon a scire facias against Maj. Edm. Bowman was referred to the next court. (p. 65)

Several persons had been summoned to appear to answer presentments at this court, but they failed to appear. Ordered that the sheriff resummon them to appear at the next court. (p. 65)

At the petition of Mr. Jno. Mikell, Sr., who married the widow (and administratress) of Mr. Jno. Culpeper, it was ordered that Frans. Lord's book of clerk's fees, now in the hands of Arthur Robins, be secured and produced at the next court. The sheriff was ordered to see that it was done. (p. 66)

Col. Littleton exited the court. (p. 66)

Col. Littleton, in behalf of himself and the county, sued Jno. Cropper. The sheriff summoned Owen Jackson and John Fawset as evidence, but they failed to attend. Ordered that they each pay Littleton 350 lbs tobacco and court costs for their contempt. (p. 66)

Christopher Thompson sued Richard Johnson, Sr., "in an action of the case" but did not file a petition; a nonsuit was granted against Thompson, who was also to pay court costs.
Christopher Thompson sued Richard Johnson, Sr., for a debt but did not file a petition; a nonsuit and court costs was granted against Thompson. (p. 66)

Jon. Goodman proved with his oath and a certificate signed by Capt. Wm. Whittington, his commander, that he fought in the King's service at James City against the rebels; Goodman, however, had not received pay. Ordered that he be given a certificate for the next assembly. (p. 66)

Maj. Edm. Bowman made it appear (by the attestation of Maj. Jno. West) that he had killed and found salt and casks for 1312 lbs of beef. Ordered that Bowman be given a certificate for the next assembly. (p. 66)

A certificate for the next assembly was granted to Tho. Barret, who swore that he served under Maj. Jno. West in the King's service for 33 days and had received no pay. (p. 67)

A certificate for the next assembly was granted at the petition of Maj. Jno. West on behalf of himself and 44 men which spent 34 days under the command of Governor Sir Wm. Berkely in the King's service at James City. (p. 67)

A certificate for the next assembly was granted to Mrs. Tabitha Browne for 370 lbs of beef; Maj. West attested that he had taken it for the Governor and country's service. (p. 67)

Jno. Stratton, who had been empowered by Governor Wm. Berkeley to procure necessary provisions, certified that he had killed a steer belonging to Frans. Wharton. Signed 15 October 1676, John Stratton, commissary. Stratton made oath to this certificate 14 September 1677. The court granted Wharton a certificate for the next assembly. (p. 67)

Jno. Cropper, who was empowered by Col. Southy Littleton to impress beef for the country's service in November 1676, spent 42 days thus employed with his horse but had received no payment except the two hides and offal he made use of from Mr. Rich. Bally. Cropper petitioned for a certificate for the assembly for payment for his time and trouble, and the court granted it. (p. 67, 68)

Ordered that all county highway surveyors go to the nearest magistrate to inform him of the places where the people should meet for clearing and mending the highways and bridges. The magistrates were to direct warrants to the constables in the precincts and summon all male tithables within the precincts to meet at the appointed places on 22 October and to bring the necessary tools and provisions to finish the work. The surveyors were to give a report of delinquent persons, who would be answerable for their contempt at the next court. If the offender was a servant, the master or mistress would be summoned. (p. 68)

Ordered that the court be adjourned to 15 (sic) November. [The records] were examined in open court September 14, 1677, signed by, Col. Southy Littleton, Maj. Jno. West, Mr. Jno. Wise, Mr. Rich. Bally, and Mr. Jno. Wallop. (p. 68)

Accomack County Court--19 November 1677

"This day the Honorable Governor's Herbert Jeffreys, Esq., commission for the peace was published in open court and ordered to be recorded."

Present: Col. Southy Littleton   Maj. Jno. West
                Capt. Charles Scarburgh   Capt. Edm. Scarburgh (p. 68)

Herbert Jeffreys, Governor of Virginia, was required (by an enactment of 28 June 1642, and act of assembly of 2 March 1661) to appoint eight honest persons as county justices and commissioners for monthly courts. Those commissioned were to take the oaths of allegiance and supremacy. Governor Jeffreys appointed the following to the quorum: Col. Southy Littleton, Mr. Charles Scarburgh, Maj. Jno. West and Capt. Daniel Jenifer. Others commissioned as justices of the peace were: Mr. Edm. Bowman, Mr. Wm. Custis, Mr. Hugh Yeo, Mr. Edward Revell, Mr. Edmund Scarburgh, Mr. Richard Hill, Mr. John Drumond, Mr. Richard Bally, Mr. Obedience Johnson and Mr. Hillary Stringer. All members or any four of them (including one member of the quorum) were empowered to act according to English law as justices of the peace to determine controversies, take depositions, take examinations and inflict punishment upon offenders, except for the taking of life and limb. The clerk of the court was required to keep records of all judgments and controversies. Signed 5 November 1677, Herb. Jeffreys. Recorded 5 December 1677, by Jno. Washbourne. (p. 69, 70)

Mr. Thomas Teackle had formerly obtained a judgment for 7148 lbs tobacco (it being public dues) against Mr. Jno. Mikael, Sr., who had married Mary the widow (and administratress) of Mr. Jno. Culpeper. Teakle petitioned that the order be reversed, since Mr. Mikael presented his account to the court making it appear that only 4182 lbs tobacco remained. Ordered that Mikael pay 4182 lbs tobacco and court costs; the remainder was to be paid as assets came into his hands. (p. 70)

Col. Littleton exited the court for the following action:
Mr. Jno. Mikael, Sr., who had married the widow (and administratress) of Mr. Jno. Culpeper, petitioned the court saying that Frans. Lord, recent deputy county clerk under Mr. Culpeper, gave Littleton several fees to collect, which were to remain in the possession of Littleton till "a certain right appeared." Ordered that Littleton pay half the fees he had received to Mikael and half to Lord. (p. 71)

Mr. Jno. Drumond took the oath of allegiance and supremacy along with the oath of commissioner. (p. 71)

Mr. Drumond entered the court. (p. 71)

Jno. Jones obtained an attachment from Capt. Rich. Hill against the estate of Thomas Barnes and claimed that Barnes owed him 2318 lbs tobacco. Since the attachment had not been served, it was ordered that it stand good and judgment would be deferred till the next court. Jones was to have priority of judgment on the estate of Barnes that could be found in the county. (p. 71)

Capt. Scarburgh exited the court and Maj. Bowman entered. (p. 71)

A proclamation was made that all housekeepers and freeholders, in obedience to the act of assembly, select a convenient place for the removal of the courthouse. All concerned persons were to appear at the first day of the next court on 16 December at the present courthouse at Pungoteage to vote. Ordered that the court clerk give copies of the proclamation to the vestry to be published in the churches so everyone could be notified. (p. 71)

Capt. Hill exited the court. (p. 71)

19 NOVEMBER 1677

Richard Hill petitioned that Thomas Willy (deceased) had left his orphaned son Tho. Willy in the care of Hill, who now promised to maintain the child with no charges to the parish. Ordered that Tho. Willy (aged 5 years) be bound to Hill till reaching the age of 18 years. Hill was enjoined not to transport the child from the county without permission. (p. 71)

Mr. Jno. West exited the court. (p. 72)

Jno. Hawes petitioned against his master Maj. Jno. West for his freedom corn and clothes, but West alleged that he could prove at the next court that Hawes had not served his legal time. Ordered that the case be referred to the next court and that Hawes return to this master's service till then. If West did not prove his allegation, Hawes would be paid for his extra time of service with corn and clothes. (p. 72)

Dorothy Watts had been bound over to this court (at the recognizance of Mr. Jno. Wallop) for breaking the peace against Rebecca Benston. Dorothy appeared in court and requested to be discharged; noting that she "stood upon" her statement, the court ordered that proclamation be made three times. As there was no objection against her, Dorothy was acquitted, but was to pay court costs. (p. 72)

Ordered that Mr. Geo. Nich. Hack be surveyor of the highways in place of Mr. Robt. Huchinson and accordingly clear the roads in that precinct. (p. 72)

Mr. Roger Mikell acknowledged that he was willing to continue as surveyor of the highways for the ensuing year. (p. 72)

Ordered that Thomas Barret continue as surveyor for the ensuing year and accordingly clear the highways in his precincts as ordered on 18 February 1675/76. (p. 72)

Ordered that Woodman Stokely continue as surveyor and that he clear the highways in his precincts as ordered 18 February 1675/76. (p. 72)

Ordered that Wm. Parker be surveyor of the highways in the place of Jno. Sturgis for the Sea Side parts of that precinct (the division was the main road) as ordered 18 February 1675/76. (p. 72)

It was ordered that Thomas Bagwell be surveyor of the highways in the place of Wm. Burton for the Sea Side parts of Roger Mikel's present precinct (the division was the main road) as ordered 18 February 1675/76. (p. 72)

Ordered that Mr. Arth. Robins be surveyor of the highways in place of Tho. Parramore. (p. 72)

The roads in the two upper precincts of the county had not been cleared through some misunderstanding. Ordered that the [residents] meet on 30 December clear the main road on the Sea Side to Gengoteige and to Maryland and the road to Jno. Rennie's. (p. 73)

In a petition to Governor Herbt. Jeffreyes, Jno. Wallop complained that when the burgesses were ordered to send the governor a list of all magistrates, his name was omitted through negligence or on purpose. To avoid a scandal on his integrity and to maintain rights in the county, Wallop wanted the governor to know of the omission and be aware that he had done nothing wrong to deserve it. Presented by Jno. Wallop, the petition was recorded on 20 November 1677, by Jno. Washbourne. (p. 73)

In an act of the assembly on 20 February 1676/77, it was ordered that the county justices meet every May and November at the courthouse to assess and set the rate on liquors according to the "market price rules." Accordingly, the price for innkeepers "to buy" was set: rum at 30 lbs per gallon; brandy at 50 lbs per gallon; Spanish [wine] at 50 lbs per gallon; French and Portugal [wine] at 40 lbs per gallon; and sugar as ordered by the court on 19 June 1677. (p. 73)

As ordered on 14 September 1677, the estate of Wm. Eborne (deceased) was appraised. It included six horses, two cattle, blankets, rugs, an Indian matchcoat, feather beds and pillows, furniture, a Bible and three other books, kitchen utensils, and tools to the value of 7584 lbs tobacco. Signed by, Jno. Parkes, Giles Cope, Arthur Robins and Jno. Cob. The appraisal was presented to the court 20 November 1677, by Arthur Robins. (p. 74)

Arthur Robins petitioned that John Hanson, merchant of Accomack County, had lately died intestate and left no relatives "in these parts" to care for his estate. Hanson was indebted to Robins, who requested to administer the estate on 20 November 1677. (p. 74, 75)

Accomack County Court--21 November 1677

Present: Col. Southy Littleton   Maj. Edm. Bowman
Capt. Charles Scarburgh   Capt. Wm. Custis
Maj. Jno. West [who then exited] (p. 75)

Wm. Smith confessed a judgment of 10,000 lbs tobacco due to Maj. Jno. West. Ordered that Smith pay the debt and court costs. (p. 75)

Jno. Cole declared that an orphan boy named John Baker, who was born on the other side of the Bay, was idle with no settled residence and had a sore leg. Cole presented Jno. Baker to the court and requested that Baker might be put to work. With Baker's consent, it was ordered that Cole care for Baker, who was to serve Cole for three years. Cole was to "use his utmost endeavor" to cure the lame leg as soon as possible and provide sufficient food, drink, clothing and shelter. At the expiration of the term, Baker was to have corn and clothes according to the custom. Cole paid court charges. (p. 75)

Capt. Hill entered the court. (p. 75)

At the last court Wm. Burntsides sued Mr. Wm. Whittington for 8036 lbs tobacco and an order passed against Jno. Cole (attorney: Mr. Tankard) for Whittington's appearance. Since Burntsides failed to appear to prosecute, the proclamation was read three times, the order against Cole was reversed and the suit was dismissed. (p. 75)

At the last court James Renny sued Jno. Renny for 5615 lbs tobacco. After proclamation was made three times, and with Jno. Renny not appearing, it was ordered that the judgment pass against the sheriff if Jno. Renny did not appear at the next court. (p. 76)

At the last court John Cole sued Robt. Watson, Sr., for 1969 lbs tobacco, and an order was passed against Mr. James Tuck for the appearance of Watson, who at this court admitted the judgment due to Jno. Cole. Ordered that Watson pay the debt and court costs; the order against Tuck was reversed. (p. 76)

The suit of Jno. Stratton (on behalf of Tho. Stokely) against Jno. Stokely, Jr., in an action of trespass, was dismissed. (p. 76)

Thomas Hall sued John Cropper (attorney: Mr. Amb. White), whom the sheriff could not find, but upon proclamation, Cropper's attorney appeared. Hall, not expecting his appearance, admitted being unprepared to prosecute the suit and requested the case be referred to the next court, which was granted with the consent of the defendant. (p. 76)

Maj. Bowman exited the court for the following action:
On 18 December 1676, Maj. Edm. Bowman had obtained an order for taking care of the estate of John Hogben (deceased) until time for administration. Upon Bowman's petition, it was ordered that William Freeman, William Martiall, John Bagwell and William Parker appraise Hogben's estate and bring an inventory to the next court. (p. 76)

The law encouraging Englishmen to kill wolves, bears, wildcats and panthers was repealed; only 150 lbs tobacco per head would be allowed to Indians who could prove they had killed any of the above creatures. (p. 76)

At the last court Mr. Richard Bally sued Jno. Cropper (attorneys: Mr. Amb. White and Mr. Tankard) for 350 lbs tobacco for hides and tallow from two oxen killed for the use of the public by virtue of Cropper's commission. The court examined the pleas on both sides and ordered that Cropper pay 200 lbs tobacco and court costs. (p. 77)

Accomack County Court--22 November 1677

Present: Col. Southy Littleton
Maj. John West   Capt. Wm. Custis
Maj. Edm. Bowman   Capt. Richard Hill (p. 77)

Jane Willis, by the oaths of Abraham Tayler and Jone Frankling, made it appear to the court that Ann (wife of James Ewell) had broken the peace by beating and assaulting Jane. Ordered that Ann Ewell be taken into the sheriff's custody until posting security for her good behavior to everyone, but especially to Jane Willis. Ann was to pay court costs. (p. 77)

John Willis and his wife were summoned to court by Nathaniel Bradford as witnesses; they had attended four days and had not been paid. Ordered that Bradford pay them 320 lbs tobacco and court charges. (p. 77)

In the suit of John Anderson against James Guy (being over a refusal to answer against the sheriff for the appearance of Guy), Wm. Anderson, attorney for Jno. Anderson, consented to refer the case to the next court. (p. 77)

Deposition of James Wathan aged about 37 years: Last January James Guy rented a sloop from Jno. Anderson for 1800 lbs tobacco per month to serve the ketch *Freanx*; Guy promised that Sheriff Tho. Walker of Somerset County would pay for it. When the sloop lay beside the ketch, Guy urged its master to load the sloop and send it "on the employ" or else to return it to Anderson, because it lay on Guy's account to pay for the hire. Signed 22 November 1677, James Wathin. (p. 77)

John West (in the court of levy) required reasonable pay for his charges in being elected a burgess to the March assembly. He had been rejected, but supposed that he should be paid at least 3000 lbs tobacco, which had been appointed by consent of the court. It was little more than two burgesses' charges, considering that Capt. Custis had "so much less by order of the last assembly." Those resisting West's request were Mr. White and Mr. Wallop. Signed, John West, who presented the above writing to the court on 22 November 1677, and requested that the clerk attest to it, which was granted by the court. The court allowed it to be recorded with the consent of West at the request of Mr. John Wallop. (p. 78)

Accomack County Court--23 November 1677

Present: Col. Southy Littleton   Maj. Edm. Bowman
Capt. William Custis   Mr. Richard Bally. (p. 78)

Margret Rickman, presented by the church wardens for fornication and bastard bearing, swore that Alexander Dun was the father. Her master John Cole agreed to post security for the payment of her fine and to save the parish from supporting the child. Ordered that Cole pay the sum and court charges. (p. 78)

Maj. Bowman exited the court and Mr. Drumond entered. (p. 78)

Elizabeth Peacock was presented by the church wardens for fornication and bastard bearing. As Maj. Edm. Bowman entered himself as security for the payment of the fine and to save the parish from supporting the child, he was ordered to pay 500 lbs tobacco and court costs. (p. 78)

Maj. Bowman and Capt. Charles Scarburgh entered the court. (p. 79)

Margret Hill was presented by the church wardens for fornication and bastard bearing. As Robt. Huchinson entered himself security for the payment of her fine and to save the parish from supporting the child, he was ordered to pay 500 lbs tobacco and court costs. (p. 79)

Maj. Jno. West entered the court. (p. 79)

John Cole's suit against Japhet Cooke was referred to the next court. (p. 79)

John Cole sued Thomas Gittings for 2071 lbs tobacco, but Gittings failed to appear. If he failed to plead at the next court, the sheriff was to pay the debt and court costs. (p. 79)

Mathew Shipp sued James Atkinson but did not appear to prosecute; the suit was dismissed. (p. 79)

Alexder. Gibson sued Lt. Col. Jno. Tillny for assault and battery but Tillny failed to appear. It was ordered that if Tilney did not answer Gibson's suit at the next court, then the sheriff would have to make satisfaction and pay court costs.

Deposition of Tho. Johnson aged about 27 years: On 27 September, Johnson was at Lt. Col. Jno. Tilny's house when Alexander Gibson came. After some discussion between them, Tilny commanded Gibson to leave the house. Tillny struck several blows on Gibson, who had in no way provoked it. Then, while Gibson was stooping down, Tilny picked up a tobacco stick (or one like it) and with both hands struck a great blow on Gibson's back. Signed 23 November 1677, Thomas Johnson.

Deposition of Mary Bell aged about 36 years: On 27 September, at the house of Lt. Col. Jno. Tinly (sic), Mary saw Tillny strike a great blow with a large stick on the back of Gibson, who was stooping over. Signed 23 November 1677, Mary (her mark) Bell. (p. 79)

The suit of Nathanl. Bradford (attorney: Mr. Tankard) against Xopher. Sadbury was referred to the next court. (p. 80)

The suit of Charles Parkes (attorney: Mr. Tankard) against Maj. Edm. Bowman was referred to the next court. (p. 80)

23 NOVEMBER 1677

The suit of Maj. Edm. Bowman against Charles Parkes was referred to the next court. (p. 80)

The suit of Mr. Tho. Welburn against Jno. Davis (attorney: Mr. White) was referred to the next court. (p. 80)

Eliz. Macin, Eliz. Man, Mary Ballard, Margt. Rycon and Rebecca Knight were presented for fornication and bastard bearing; they had been summoned to this court but failed to appear. Ordered that the sheriff immediately take them into his custody till they gave security to appear at the next court. (p. 80)

Col. Littleton exited the court for the following:
Col. Sou. Littleton's suit against Jno. Cropper was referred to the next court. (Attorneys: Mr. Amb. White and Mr. Tankard).
Deposition of Wm. Fawset aged about 16 years: Last spring Wm. heard John Cropper order his servants Jno. Coulston and Joseph Woodland to drive about 19 head of Rhody Fawset's cattle to the head of John Fawset's land and wait for Cropper. When he arrived, the servants took the cattle to Maryland. Signed 23 November 1677, Wm. (W) Fawset. (p. 80)

The suit of Mr. Wm. Anderson upon a scire facias against Mr. Edm. Bowman was referred to the next court. (p. 80)

Wm. Tayler, Sr., was bound by Mr. Jno. Wallop's recognizance to answer for assaulting and beating Masseteage and his wife, Indians belonging to Occasonson. The Indians proved the beating, but Tayler exhibited a complaint against the Indians for killing his hogs. Ordered that the complaint on both sides be dismissed with each paying their own charges. (p. 80)

Wm. Fawset was granted his choice of a guardian, Richard Kellum, Sr., who was to care for Wm. and his estate after giving security to be answerable for the estate when Fawset came of age. (p. 81)

John Stratton admitted that on 6 February 1676/77, at an election of burgesses, in the hearing of several persons he said that Col. Southy Littleton was a mutineer and used other disparaging words. Acknowledging this to be scandalous and abusive to Littleton, Stratton expressed his sorrow, submitting himself and promising to pay the charges in a suit arising from the incident. Signed 23 November 1677, John Stratton. The above was acknowledged in open court by Stratton, at which Littleton acquitted him. (p. 81)

On behalf of himself and the public, Wm. Custis petitioned against James Ewel for unlawfully killing cattle. After examining several depositions, the jury found Ewel guilty and ordered him to pay 500 lbs tobacco to the public and 500 lbs tobacco to the informer. He was to remain in the sheriff's custody till giving security for his good behavior and paying court costs.

The jury considered all evidence against James Ewell and found him guilty of unlawfully killing cattle. Signed 23 November 1677, Wm. Anderson, foreman.

Deposition of Nathan Bradford and Rich. Frankling: Some time in October they went with the constable to search James Ewel's house by virtue of a warrant from Capt. Wm. Custis. In the house they found beef both "hung and green" from several four or five year old animals, judging by the bones. They also found parts of several hides, one of which had been killed only eight or nine days before. The head and ears [with distinguishing marks] had been cut off. Signed 23 November 1677, Nathaniel Bradford and Richard Frankling.

Deposition of John Willis and Jane: John and Jane were neighbors of James Ewell and well acquainted with his cattle; in the past two years they knew of no cattle raised by him except for two heifers. One died a year ago, the other was a cow now living. All others had been killed or died at about a year of age. Several times during the summer and fall the Willis' dog brought home a muzzle or skin or nose of a cow, and once the horns and head of a beast. They also saw some beef, dried and fresh, in Ewel's house. Signed 23 November 1677, Jno. (E) Willis and Jane (K) Willis.

Deposition of Richard Frankling: James Ewell agreed to pay Frankling a cow and calf in place of the cow that Frankling charged Ewell of unlawfully killing. Sworn in open court 23 November 1677.

James Youell admitted and bound himself to pay 10,000 lbs tobacco (on the Bay Side) to Nathaniel Bradford and Richard Franklin upon demand. Signed James (I) Youel.

Condition of the above obligation: if James Youell saved Nathl. Bradford and Rich. Frankling from any suit arising as by virtue of a warrant from Capt. Wm. Custis and a commitment of James Ewell, then the obligation was to stand in full force. Otherwise it would be void. Signed, James Youel. Witnesses: Jno. Stratton and Tho. Barrit.

James Youel bound himself to pay Richard Frankling one good cow and calf on the last of April within seven miles of Matchepungo. Signed 23

November 1677, James (I) Youel. Witnesses: John Stratton and Tho. Barret. (p. 81-83)

Mr. William Anderson in behalf of orphan Eliz. Smith was granted a judgment of 2146 lbs tobacco against Jno. Stokely, it being half of the nine hogsheads of tobacco made on the plantation of Edwd. Smith (deceased). (p. 83)

On 23 November 1677, [the records] were examined in open court. Ordered that the court be adjourned till 17 December. Signed by Jno. Washbourne. (p. 83)

Accomack County Court--17 December 1677

Present: Col. Southy Littleton   Mr. Jno. Drumond
             Maj. John West   Maj. Edm. Bowman (p. 84)

Capt. Daniel Jenifer, high sheriff, informed the court that the sheriff of Northampton had forcibly entered Accomack County and seized several hogsheads of tobacco as taxes for Northampton County. Ordered that Capt. Daniel Jenifer collect the levies in that part of the county and seize the tobacco collected by Northampton's sheriff. While discharging the inhabitants, he was to give the Governor notice and get his order to stop such illegal proceedings until a trial. Col. Wm. Kendall of Northampton desired a meeting of both courts to settle the difference. Accomack County was willing in spite of the "great breach of friendship and neighbourhood" to meet at any time and place near the bounds of the county. (p. 84)

Richard Johnson, Sr., obtained two orders of nonsuit against Christopher Thomson on 14 September for not appearing to prosecute. Thomson now petitioned saying that he thought the court was to be held on 17 September and therefore failed to prosecute. Johnson had taken out executions on the nonsuits; ordered that the sheriff suspend them till further order. (p. 84)

Margeret Rydon was presented by the church wardens for fornication and bastard bearing. Since Peter Parker entered himself as security to pay her fine, it was ordered that he pay 500 lbs tobacco and court charges. (p. 85)

Maj. West exited the court for the following action:
Elizabeth Man was presented by the church wardens for fornication and bastard bearing. Since Edward Brotherton entered himself as security to pay her fine, it was ordered that Brotherton pay 500 lbs tobacco and court charges. (p. 85)

Accomack County Court--18 December 1677

Present: Col. Southy Littleton   Capt. Wm. Custis
              Maj. Edm. Bowman   Capt. Edm. Scarburgh (p. 85)

Wm. Tayler, Sr., petitioned to be paid for two of his servants giving evidence at the last court for the Occaconson Indians. Since the witnesses were summoned on behalf of the King, the court felt that Tayler should not have payment; the suit was dismissed. (p. 85)

At the June court Samuel Tayler received an order for 560 lbs tobacco against Joseph Lineger's estate. Since his last year's taxes were 66 lbs tobacco, and since Tayler requested respite because one of his witnesses did not appear, it was ordered that the sheriff pay Tayler 626 lbs tobacco and court costs. (p. 85)

Charles Holden, attorney of Jno. Davis, confessed a judgment of 1050 lbs tobacco due to Mr. Thomas Welburne. Ordered that Davis pay the debt and court costs. (p. 85)

John Davis authorized Mr. Ambrose White or Mr. Charles Holden to appear at the next court for him at the suit of Mr. Thomas Welburne, merchant, and confess a judgment of 1050 lbs tobacco and costs. Signed 16 September 1677, John (I) Davis. Witnesses: Soustian Delastatis and Ben Eyre. Sworn in open court 17 December 1677, by Benja. Eyre. (p. 86)

A certificate for the next assembly was granted to Robert Hill, who swore that he served the recent Governor William Berkeley under the orders of Maj. John West for one month and four days in killing meat for the government's use. He also served 11 days during the time of the rebellion. (p. 86)

18 DECEMBER 1677

A certificate for the next assembly was granted to Joseph Nuton and John Bishop, who swore that they served for 11 days in a shallop as soldiers under the command of Col. Littleton during the rebellion. (p. 86)

A certificate for the next assembly was granted to Jno. Collins, who swore that he served for 30 days during the rebellion under the command of Capt. Wm. Whittington, and also nine days watching on the Bay Side. (p. 86)

A certificate for the next assembly was granted to Thomas Evans, who swore that he served a total of 20 days during the rebellion: nine days in a shallop under Col. Littleton, nine days in the sloop *Wm. & Ann*, and two days guarding the prisoners. (p. 86)

According to the petition of Edmond Joynes, the mother of the orphan Jon. Hinderson (heir of Gilbert Hinderson), on her deathbed requested that her son be raised by Joynes. The orphan, who wished to remain in Joynes' custody, was ordered to remain with Joynes till coming of age. Joynes was to take charge of the estate, provided he build one 20 foot square house, plant and tend 100 apple trees, make a cornfield containing 4000 hills of corn, teach the orphan to read and pay court costs. [In an apparent error, the orphan was once called "Gilbt" in this record.] (p. 87)

Joseph Nuton petitioned the court: Mary Chapwell (once the widow of Wm. Eborne) had been given charge of Sara Eborne, but Mary had since died. Now Nuton desired to have charge of Sara. Ordered that Sara Eborne remain with Jno. Collins till the next court, to which Collins was to bring her.

Arthur Robins petitioned to have charge of Henry Eborne, since Mary, the wife of Tho. Chapell, before her death requested that Robins take care of Henry. Ordered that Henry Eborne remain under the care of Robins till coming of age.

Arthur Frame stated that since the death of Mary, the wife of Thomas Chappel, he had taken into his care Rebecca, the daughter of Wm. Eborne (deceased). Frame was granted custody of Rebecca and promised that if his future ability allowed it, he would teach Rebecca Eborne to read "as far forth as his own children." Frame paid court costs.

John Reade stated that he had cared for Ann, daughter of Wm. and Mary Eborne, for three years with the consent of her father and mother. Since her parents were both dead, Reade declared himself willing to keep Ann until she came of age. If his future ability allowed it, he promised to teach her to read as far as his own children. Ordered that Ann remain in the care of Reade, who also paid court charges. (p. 87)

Mr. John Wallop petitioned to be paid for attending court five days as a witness for Col. Littleton against Mr. Jno. Stratton. Since Stratton obliged himself to pay all charges arising in the suit, it was ordered that he pay 200 lbs tobacco to Wallop along with the court costs. (p. 88)

Mary Ballard, servant to Mr. Tho. Teackle, was presented for fornication and bastard bearing; she named Rich. Price, servant to John Cropper, as the father. Ordered that Mary be taken into the sheriff's custody and receive 29 lashes on the bare back unless she could find sufficient security to pay 500 lbs tobacco and court charges before the court adjourned. (p. 88)

Rebecca Knight was presented by the church wardens for fornication and bastard bearing. Mr. James Matts, her master, agreed to pay her fine and to save the parish from the cost of child support. Ordered that he pay 500 lbs tobacco and court charges. (p. 88)

Richard Bundock, Sr., had obtained an attachment against the estate of Jno. Tarr; it was returned on tobacco, a cow and calf and a mare belonging to Tarr's estate and now in the hands of Wm. Wyatt. Bundock declared that Tarr owed him 1450 lbs tobacco, but could not immediately prove his claim. Ordered that the case be referred to the next court so the claim could be proved. (p. 88)

Arthur Robins petitioned the court saying that the administration of the estate of Wm. Eborne (deceased) had been granted to Tho. Chappell in the right of his wife. The estate had been appraised, but Chappell could not put in security as required by law. Since Chappell's wife had since died, it was ordered that administration be granted to Robins, who was to post security. (p. 88)

Jno. Anderson had sued James Guy for 1200 lbs tobacco, and an order was passed against the sheriff for the appearance of Guy. Since both parties consented to refer the case to the next court, it was so ordered. (p. 89)

James Steavens, "covenant servant" to Capt. Edm. Scarburgh, petitioned for his freedom but did not prove his case; the suit was dismissed. (p. 89)

18 DECEMBER 1677

Jno. Stokely made it appear that he had paid debts of 544 lbs tobacco for Edward Smith (deceased). Ordered that the above sum be deducted from the judgment of 2146 lbs tobacco obtained by Mr. Wm. Anderson on behalf of Eliz. Smith, orphan. Anderson was to pay court costs. (p. 89)

Certificate was granted to Mr. Thomas Welburne for 200 acres for transporting:
Ben. Eyre   Tho. Welburne   (p. 89)
Wm. Sill   Jno. Welburne

Accomack County Court--19 December 1677

Present: Maj. Gen. John Custis
       Col. Southy Littleton   Maj. Edm. Bowman
       Maj. Jno. West   Capt. Wm. Custis (p. 89)

Mr. Edward Revell's servant boy named George Davis was judged to be 17 years old and was ordered to serve accordingly. (p. 89)

The commission of the court was "very much altered, and several magistrates removed from their ancient places, which hath caused some discontent and several magistrates hath refused to sit in court." As Capt. Charles Scarburgh and Maj. Jno. West declared that it was caused by mistake, the court requested that Maj. Gen. Jno. Custis inform the Governor and entreat him to send a new commission "according to everyone's ancient place." Ordered that the clerk give Custis a copy of the old commission and other orders for the placing of the court. (p. 89)

At the last court Alexander Gibson sued Lt. Col. Jno. Tillny for assault and battery, and an order was passed against the sheriff for Tillny's appearance. The sheriff produced Tillny, who alleged that Gibson abused him first, and what Tillny did, he did as an officer in his own defense. Tillny was granted his requested to bring proof to the next court so a final determination could be made. (p. 90)

Nic. Millechop admitted owing 8000 lbs tobacco to Capt. Daniel Jenifer, who was going to sue Millechop at the next court. Millechop empowered his attorney to confess the judgment. Signed 15 December 1677, Nic. Millechop. Any one of the following attorneys would do: Mr. Ambrose White, Mr. Jno. Tankard or Mr. Charles Holden. Signed by Jno. Belmaine. (p. 90)

Charles Holden, attorney of Nich. Millechop, confessed a judgment of 8000 lbs tobacco due to Capt. Daniel Jenifer. Ordered that Millechop pay the debt and court costs. (p. 90)

The suit of Col. South. Littleton against Jno. Cropper was referred to the next court. (p. 90)

Maj. West exited the court for the following action:
The case of Jno. Hawes was referred to this court, where Maj. Jno. West was to prove his claim of further service. West, however, did not have proof, so it was ordered that Hawes have his freedom corn and clothes and court costs. (p. 90)

Maj. Bowm[an] exited the court for the following action:
On 18 September 1676, Mr. Wm. Anderson obtained an order against Maj. Edm. Bowman. Ordered that the judgment be revived for further process. (p. 90)

At the last court John Cole sued Thomas Gittings for 2071 lbs tobacco; order was passed against the sheriff for Gittings' appearance, and since he had not produced him to answer the charges, Cole desired a confirmation against the sheriff. Ordered that the sheriff pay the debt and court costs. (p. 91)

Nath. Bradford (attorney: Mr. Tankred) sued Christopher Sadbury for defamation. Sadbury was called to court but acknowledged himself to be too drunk to answer the suit; ordered that Sadbury be fined 50 lbs tobacco and that the suit be referred to the next court. (p. 91)

The complaint of Joseph Nuton against Grubbing Hoe Indian was dismissed; the court found no cause for action. (p. 91)

Accomack County Court--20 December 1677

Present: Col. Southy Littleton   Maj. Edm. Bowman
               Maj. John West   Capt. Wm. Custis (p. 91)

The suit of Thomas Hall against Jno. Cropper was referred to the next court; ordered that the sheriff take security from Cropper to answer the suit and pay all costs and damages. Cropper was to answer in writing at least a day before the next court. (p. 91)

20 DECEMBER 1677

Deposition of Wm. Fauset aged about 16 years: Thomas Hall's servant named Richard Price came into Jno. Cropper's corn field where Fauset was working. When Price, who had a big club in his hand, asked for Cropper, "We did tell him that Jno. Cropper was at work topping off tobacco." After Price and Cropper talked a little while, they returned, and Cropper told his maid servant to go into the house and give "that fellow" some food. Then Cropper said that he dared not entertain him. Fauset knew nothing more of their secret dealings, but saw Price there several times. "One time I was sent by Cropper to his barn to carry the said Richard one quart of milk and cider, and several times the said Cropper gave all of us charges that we should not tell that Rich. Price was there." Fauset was told that Cropper transported Price behind him on his horse to Richd. Hill's and told Price to go in there and they would "take him up." Cropper told Price to say "that he was at a long bridge and that he should inquire the way to Pokehetenorton and that he had seen a brick house and that he saw people going from court." Fauset had gotten this information from Richard Price and Joseph Woodland. Signed 21 November 1677, Wm. (W) Fawset. Sworn in open court 20 December 1677.

Deposition of Ann Fox aged about 22 years: On a Thursday about the middle of last August, Ann was working in John Cropper's corn field with his other servants. (At that time she was also his servant.) Richard Price, servant to Thomas Hall, asked where "our master was." Price said he wanted to speak with Cropper and asked if they had seen a strange horse, which they had not. They offered to call their master; instead, Price wanted directions to find him. Very shortly Price returned with Cropper, who commanded Ann, Wm. Fosset, Charles Fosset and a servant called Joseph "to be sure not to tell any person" that Rich. Price was there; they were not to tell his master or anyone else that "we had so much as seen him." Cropper told Ann to go and get Price some food, and when they had been inside a short time, Cropper came and told Price that "he would not by any means have anyone see him there but he told him he might go into the barn and lie there upon the wheat and that he should have victuals and might come into that house at night when he was gone to bed."

The next morning around breakfast time, Price came out of the barn and went into the house; he requested Cropper to go to court, and try to buy him from Tho. Hall, his master. Cropper said he would buy Price if he could, even if it cost him two servants. So that Friday, Cropper went to court, but returned that night saying that "there was a hue and cry out for the apprehending of him, and that he had spoken with his master, but that he would not yield to sell him. The said Richard was in a great chase and said he would never serve Tho. Hall, but would go as far as a pair of shoes would carry him or hang himself first." Cropper said that Price's master "had promised to be there with him next morning and did not question but at long run to make a bargain."

The next day Cropper "went from home into the lower county (as he said)"; he told Ann to feed Price and not let anyone know he was there. When Cropper returned on Monday evening, Ann told him that Tho. Hall and his wife had been there that morning to see Cropper and requested that he come to their house. When Cropper asked if Ann had seen Richard since his master had been there, she directed him to the orchard. Cropper "went towards the barn into the orchard" and then left immediately to go to Mrs. Fosset's.

The next morning he came home and asked what "Tho. Hall had said and whether I was willing to serve him. I replied I was willing to serve him provided you will clothe me well." The next Wednesday Cropper took Ann to Hall's, where she heard Hall ask Cropper if he knew anything about Richard. When Cropper said no, Hall said he would bet 500 lbs tobacco that he was lying. Cropper offered to swear before any commissioner that he "did not know anything of him or had ever seen him since his running away."

When Price came during Cropper's absence, he asked the servants not to tell Cropper that he was there; when they demurred, he replied that it didn't matter; Cropper himself did not want them to tell him.

As Cropper was bringing Ann to Hall's house, he asked her not to tell anything about him and Rich. Price and promised "many kindnesses" to her when she was free if she did not tell.

Ann heard Price say that he had seen Hall and his wife when they came to Cropper's on Monday morning; he went out of the barn into the woods and "cut a good cudgel and was resolved to bang his said master if he had come near him." She also heard Richard say that on Monday night he "had almost discovered himself to his master before he was aware, but that he heard his master's tongue in the house just as he was ready to come in at the door." Signed 20 December 1677, Ann (AF) Fox. (p. 91-94)

Max Gore sued Edward Hamond for 2513 lbs tobacco; though proclamation was made three times, Hamond failed to appear. Ordered that judgment pass against the sheriff if Hamond did not appear at the next court. (p. 94)

Thomas Gooding sued Roger Mikell for a debt; Capt. Daniel Jenifer alleged that Mikell, who had some urgent business elsewhere, asked Jenifer to request a reference to the next court, which was granted. (p. 94)

20 DECEMBER 1677

King Robin, an Indian, petitioned that Mr. Arthur Upshot and Nathl. Bradford be summoned to appear at the next court. In the mean time the Indian (and others) were to remain on the disputed land and enjoy all the former privileges except for the shooting of guns. (p. 94)

Mr. Frans. Lord sued Mr. James Mitts, who married the executrix of Mr. George Parker, but did not appear to prosecute. The suit was dismissed. (p. 94)

Richard Kellum, Sr., guardian of Wm. Fawset, desired an order concerning the estate left Wm. by his father's will, and John Cropper acknowledged that he was willing to deliver the estate belonging to the orphan. Ordered that Cropper immediately deliver to Kellum the estate of Wm. Fauset, including any part of it that may have been transported from the county. When Kellum had received the estate, he was to give an account to the court. (p. 94)

Maj. Gen. Jno. Custis entered the court. (p. 95)

The suit of Mr. Tho. Teakle against Jno. Cropper was dismissed. (p. 95)

Col. Littleton exited the court for the following action:
William Chace confessed a judgment of 314 lbs tobacco due to Col. Southy Littleton. He was to pay the debt and court costs. (p. 95)

Maj. West exited the court for the following action:
Mr. Robt. Huchinson was granted a judgment of 3478 lbs tobacco against Jno. West. Ordered that West pay the debt and court costs. (p. 95)

Mr. Max. Gore was granted a judgment of 851 lbs tobacco against Tho. Chappell. Ordered that Chappel pay the debt and court costs. (p. 95)

Maj. West exited the court. (p. 95)

Maj. John West's suit against Garret Supple was referred to the next court. (p. 95)

Maj. Jno. West sued John Tarr (as the assignee of James Renny) for 600 lbs tobacco. Since Tarr did not appear in court, an attachment was ordered to issue against his estate wherever it could be found in the county. (p. 95)

Christopher Calvert, Sr., was granted a judgment of 1000 lbs tobacco against Richard Turner. Ordered that Turner pay the debt and court costs. (p. 95)

Wm. White's suit against Mr. Jno. Mikell was referred to the next court. (p. 95)

The suit of Henry Reade against Mr. Jno. Mikael, who married the widow and administratress of Mr. Jno. Culpeper, was referred to the next court. (p. 95)

Richard Piwell petitioned the court for pay for the five days he attended court as a witness summoned by Mr. Charles Leatherbury. Ordered that Leatherbury pay Piwell 200 lbs tobacco and court costs. (p. 96)

Henry Jenkins petitioned the court for pay for the six days he attended court as a witness summoned by Mr. Charles Leatherbury. Ordered that Leatherbury pay Jenkins 240 lbs tobacco and court costs. (p. 96)

Charles Leatherbury's complaint against Matahows and Bundick, Indians, was dismissed because there was no cause for action. (p. 96)

Deposition of Vrmston Foster aged about 27 years: Foster was with Edward Hamond, Francis Brookes and Henry Brookes on Phillip Fisher's plantation when he heard Francis Brookes and his brother agree to buy Hamond's plantation (on which Hamond was then living). The price was to be either 13,500 or 14,000 lbs tobacco and ten yards of blue linen. As earnest for the bargain, Francis and Henry Brookes gave ten yards of blue linen, 500 lbs tobacco credit at Henry Custis' store, and a yearling mare worth 1000 lbs tobacco. The land was to be paid for in two years. Signed 20 December 1677, Vrmson Foster. (p. 96)

Griffeth Savage, as church warden for the parish of Accomack, some time ago had agreed that Mrs. Ann Challton should care for a bastard child belonging to her servant at the rate of 1300 lbs tobacco per year unless other future arrangements were made. Signed 13 December 1677, Griffeth Savage. On 16 December 1677, Maj. Jno. West acknowledged the above certificate to be the act of Griff. Savage. (p. 96)

Deposition of Mary Stokely (widow and executrix of Edward Smith) aged about 24 years: She had given a complete account of the moveable estate of Edward Smith, her late husband, to Will. Andrews. All had been divided except the hogs, a heifer and a steer; nothing had been concealed. Signed 14 July 1677, by Mary Stokely, and sworn before Jno. Wallop on 18 December 1677. Recorded at the request of Mr. Wm. Anderson. (p. 97)

Deposition of Richard Holland aged about 43 years: Last September Thomas Barnet came to Holland's house and brought a pigskin saddle and two bridles. Holland knew one bridle belonged to Col. Littleton (who claimed the other one as well). Barnet offered to sell or trade the saddle for one of Holland's, but fearing it was stolen, Holland refused. Barnet also brought three or four loads of "high swan shot" and powder. Barnet said he had gotten it from Col. Littleton's servant when they were "out hunting the neck." Signed 20 December 1677, Richard (H) Holland. (p. 97)

John Cole reminded the gentlemen of Accomack County that since he came to Pungoteage, he had given the county "free liberty to keep court at my house without charging the county." Now the court was to be moved to some other place voted by the people; Cole had purchased William Freeman's plantation, which he felt was a convenient place to build a courthouse. If that place was "picked upon the major votes of the people for a courthouse to be there built, I have thirty thousand bricks, the making and burning of them due to me from James Ewell, which labor of his I will give towards the building of the said courthouse, and also what timber is convenient on the land I will also give as much as will build the said house. And further, I will fit a house up that is on the said land for the county's use to keep court in for the present whilst the county is a building there the aforesaid courthouse, and in the interim, I will be a building housing for the accommodation of those that have occasion, and if concluded by the people, as I have above mentioned, I am very willing to perform as I have aforesaid promised." Signed 17 December 1677, John Cole. Presented to the court 20 December 1677. (p. 97, 98)

Accomack County Court--17 January 1677/78

Present: Col. Southy Littleton   Maj. Edm. Bowman
Capt. Charles Scarburgh   Capt. Edm. Scarburgh (p. 98)

Mrs. Tabitha Browne petitioned that the estate of Japhet Cooke owed her 2112 lbs tobacco. She requested administration of the estate or an order against it. Her claim was recorded; if no will appeared within nine months, she was to have an order against the estate according to priority. (p. 98)

Capt. Cha. Scarburgh exited the court and Maj. West entered it. (p. 98)

Capt. Charles Scarburgh claimed that Japhet Cooke died intestate and owed him 2501 lbs tobacco. Ordered that the claim be recorded and that he have an order against the estate according to priority. (p. 98)

Thomas Hall claimed that the estate of Japhet Cooke owed him 1500 lbs tobacco. Ordered that his claim be recorded and that he have an order against the estate according to priority. (p. 99)

Robert Hardy, servant of George Smith, acknowledged that he was willing to serve Smith seven years from the time of his arrival in Virginia. (p. 99)

Mary Windham, servant of Mrs. Ann Charleton, petitioned for her freedom corn and clothes but did not prove her petition. Ordered that Mary return to Charleton's service, and since it appeared that Mary had "unjustly molested" her mistress, she was ordered to pay 50 lbs tobacco and court charges at the expiration of her term of service. (p. 99)

Richard Bundock, Sr., proved his attachment of 1451 lbs tobacco against the estate of John Tarr. The sheriff served the attachment on a black cow, a calf and a red mare; it was ordered that these satisfy the debt and court costs. (p. 99)

Capt. Edm. Scarburgh exited the court for the following action:
James Steaphans petitioned against his master, Capt. Edm. Scarburgh, for his freedom corn and clothes, but since he did not prove his case, the complaint was dismissed. (p. 99)

Jonathan Owen was granted an attachment of 2110 lbs tobacco from Col. Southy Littleton on the estate of John Tarr. Since the attachment was not returned by the sheriff at this court, it was deferred till the next court. (p. 99)

Arthur Frame declared that Rebecca Eborne, orphan of Wm. Eborne, was committed into his care, but Arthur Robins had administration of Eborne's estate. Ordered that Robins deliver the orphan's share to Frame on behalf of the orphan. (p. 100)

Jno. Read declared that Ann Eborne, orphan of Wm. Eborne, was committed into his care, but Arthur Robins had administration of Eborne's estate. Ordered that Robins deliver the orphan's share to Read on behalf of the orphan. (p. 100)

Capt. Scarburgh exited and Capt. Custis entered the court. (p. 100)

Mr. James Tuck brought to court Paul Carter's servant boy named John Hancock, who was judged to be 17 years old and was ordered to serve the term of seven years from the time of his arrival. (p. 100)

Garatt Sepell assigned power of attorney to Walter Tayler to acknowledge a judgment of 1037 lbs tobacco due to John West. Signed 17 January 1677/78, Garatt (X) Sepell. Witnesses: Wm. (W) Waite and Tho. (B) Barnet.
Walter Tayler confessed Garret Supple's judgment of 1037 lbs tobacco due to Maj. John West. Ordered that Supple pay the debt and court costs. (p. 100)

John Cropper confessed a judgment of 900 lbs tobacco due to Charles Holden. Cropper was ordered to pay the debt and court costs. (p. 101)

Arthur Upshot and Nathl. Bradford were summoned to answer the complaint of King Robin, an Indian. Since Robin could not prove his complaint, it was dismissed. (p. 101)

Deposition of Rich. Jones, Jr., aged about 23 years: Will. Simons asked Jones to write a "condition" binding him to Daniel Moccarty for the term of one year. Signed 17 January 1677/78, Rich. Jones, Jr. (p. 101)

Accomack County Court--18 January 1677/78

Present: Col. Southy Littleton   Capt. Wm. Custis
          Maj. Edm. Bowman   Capt. Edm. Scarburgh (p. 101)

Mr. Thomas Welburne sued Robt. Bracy for a debt, but at the request of Charles Holden, attorney of Bracy, the suit was referred to the next court. (p. 101)

Jno. Renny's suit against James Renny was referred to the next court. (p. 101)

Mr. Charles Holden, attorney of Walter Tayler, confessed a judgment of 1299 lbs tobacco due to Mr. Wm. Anderson. Ordered that Tayler pay the debt and court costs.

Walter Tayler appointed Mr. Cha. Houlding to confess the above judgment to William Anderson. Signed, Walter Tayler. Witnesses: Jno. Washbourne and George Charnock, who acknowledged the above act in open court on 18 January 1677/78. (p. 101, 102)

Mrs. Amy Fowkes' servant boy named Edward Wright was judged to be 16 years old and was ordered to serve accordingly. (p. 102)

Mr. Richard Bally's servant boy named Edward Hues was judged to be 15 years old and was ordered to serve accordingly. (p. 102)

Mr. Bally entered the court. (p. 102)

The suit of Nathaniel Bradford (attorney: Cha. Holden) against Christopher Sadbury for defamation had been referred to this court. Sadbury "submitted himself to the said Bradford", who accepted and discharged him. Ordered that the suit be dismissed with Sadbury paying court costs.

"I own I said that I had lost several goods, but do not remember that I said as is charged in Mr. Nathaniel Bradford's petition. If I did, I am sorry for it." Signed 18 January 1677/78, Christopher Sadbury.

Petition of Nath. Bradford: About 13 August, at Watchepregue in the hearing of several people, Xophr. Sadbury said that Bradford stole malt from him along with 50 pounds sterling worth of goods. Sadbury also said that Bradford and his wife kept the key of the room where the goods lay, and when they were done with the key, they threw it on the dunghill. Bradford was suing for 40 lbs sterling in damages. (p. 102, 103)

Maj. Jno. West, as attorney of Alexander Draper, was granted a judgment of 1600 lbs tobacco against John Renny. The debt was due by bill as security for Edward Hazard. Ordered that Renny pay the debt and court costs. (p. 103)

Capt. Ed. Scarb[urgh] exited the court and Maj. West entered. (p. 103)

John Cropper confessed a judgment of 1000 lbs tobacco due to Capt. Edmond Scarburgh. Ordered that he pay the debt and court costs. (p. 103)

18 JANUARY 1677/78

Mr. Jona Jackson, as attorney of Mr. Max. Robinson, was granted a judgment of 440 lbs tobacco against John Cropper. Ordered that Cropper pay the debt and court costs. (p. 103)

Max. Robinson of Rappahanocke County granted Mr. Jonah Jackson power of attorney to handle his affairs in Accomack and Somerset Counties, as did Mr. Jno. Haselwood, merchant of London. Signed 27 September 1677, Max. Robinson. Witnesses: John Revell and John Burrougs. (p. 103, 104)

Jno. Tanner entered an action for 580 lbs tobacco against Ralph Doe, who did not appear. Tanner was granted an attachment for the debt and court costs against Doe's estate, if it could be found in the county. (p. 104)

Maj. West exited the court for the following action:
Maj. Jno. West was granted an attachment on the estate of Jno. Tarr. As the attachment was served and returned by the sheriff "upon no certain particulars", it was referred to the next court. (p. 104)

Jno. Cole entered an action for 435 lbs tobacco against Rhodrick Powell, who failed to appear. Cole was granted an attachment with court costs against Powell's estate where it could be found in the county. (p. 104)

Alex. Gibson authorized Charles Holden to appear for him in his suit against Mr. Jno. Tilney. Signed 17 December 1677, Alex. Gibson and presented to the court by Holden on 18 January 1677/78.
Jno. Tilney authorized Jno. Tankard to appear for him in the suit of Alexander Gibson and "use your utmost endeavor for my defence." Signed 16 January 1677/78, Jno. Tilney. Witnesses: George Charnock and Davis Pearse. Presented to the court by Tankard on 18 January 1677/78.
Alexander Gibson's suit against Lt. Col. Jno. Tillny for assault and battery had been referred to this court; the case was referred to a jury which found Tillny guilty and awarded 500 lbs tobacco damages to Gibson. The court confirmed the verdict and ordered that Tillny pay that sum and court costs.

Wm. Anderson was foreman of the jury:

Robt. Atkinson	Jno. Hanning	Tho. Osburne
Jno. Bagwell	Wm. Martial	Abr. Tayler
Jno. Barnes	Bar. Meares	George West
Geo. Nich. Hack	Wm. Nock	(p. 105)

Deposition of Rich. Cox aged about 20 years: Cox was at the house of Lt. Col. Jno. Tilney with Alex. Gibson and Tho. Johnson when he heard

Tillney and Gipson "capping verses."[2] Tilney began to quarrel and ordered Gipson out of his house. Cox then saw Tillney "strike Gipson a great blow on the back with a tobacco stick or some such like." Signed 18 January 1677/78, Richard Cokes.

Deposition of Jno. Michael, Jr., aged about 34 years: At the last court, Michael heard Lt. Col. Jno. Tilney and Alexander Gibson "repeating their difference" when Gibson admitted throwing Tilney down out of doors. Signed 18 January 1677/78, Jno. Michael, Jr. (p. 105, 106)

Maximilian Gore assigned power of attorney to Mr. Ambrose White to confess a judgment totalling 115 pounds sterling to Capt. Daniel Jenifer. Signed 16 January 1677/78, Maximilian Gore. Witness: Jno. Belman.

Mr. Amb. White, as attorney for Maximilian Gore, confessed a judgment of 115 pounds sterling due to Capt. Daniel Jenifer. The debt was to be paid with protest money and court costs. (p. 106, 107)

Capt. Ed. Scarburgh and Col. Littleton exited the court and Capt. Cha. Scarb[urgh] entered. (p. 107)

Daniel Owen complained against Robt. Dungworth and John Milburne for transporting a hog without ears [which bore identifying marks]. Dungworth and Milburne were bound over by Capt. Charles Scarburgh's warrant and the court fully examined the case. Because Thomas Tayler confessed to killing the hog and asking Dungworth and Milburne to carry it to his house, he was ordered to pay the costs; the servants were dismissed. (p. 107)

The suit of Col. Littleton against John Tayler was referred to the next court. (p. 107)

Col. Littleton entered the court. (p. 107)

George West was granted an attachment of 1283 lbs tobacco against the estate of Peter Peco. It was executed on Peco's estate in the hands of Tho. Osburne, but "not on any particulars." The attachment was delayed till the next court. (p. 107)

---

[2]*In capping verses, one person quotes a verse and the other must cap it by quoting a verse beginning with the initial or final letter, the initial of the last word, or with a rhyming word, etc.*

18 JANUARY 1677/78

Mr. William Anderson entered action for 1029 lbs tobacco against Wm. Onoughton, but the sheriff could not find him. Ordered that attachment be granted against Onoughton's estate where it could be found in the county. (p. 107)

Tho. Osburne entered action for 1162 lbs tobacco against Peter Pecoeh, but the sheriff could not find him. Ordered that attachment be granted against Pecoe's estate where it could be found in the county. (p. 107)

Because Tho. Williams attended court for six days as a witness summoned by Xopher Sadbury, it was ordered that Sadbury pay Williams 240 lbs tobacco and court charges. (p. 107)

Maj. Bowman exited the court. (p. 108)

Maj. Edm. Bowman sued Tho. Gording for a debt, but Gording was granted liberty till the next court to prove it was paid. (p. 108)

Maj. Edm. Bowman, administrator of the estate of Jno. Hogben (deceased), was granted a judgment of 1012 lbs tobacco against Capt. Daniel Jenifer, who was ordered to pay the debt and court costs. (p. 108)

Wm. Anderson, attorney of John Anderson, obtained an order against the sheriff because James Guy did not appear. Guy owed Anderson 1200 lbs tobacco for the hire of a sloop. Ordered that the sheriff pay the debt and court costs. (Sidenote: The order was satisfied 8 April 1678, signed by Ben. Eyre, subsheriff.)

John Anderson, planter of Somerset County, Maryland, assigned power of attorney to Wm. Anderson, merchant, to sue James Guy, "sojourner in the said county of Accomack mariner" for 1200 lbs tobacco. Signed 12 May 1677, by John Anderson and acknowledged 25 August 1677, before Cornelius Steenacre and James Tayler. Witnesses: Walter (R) Henry, Thomas Feild and Will. Stevans.

Walter Henry and Tho. Feild swore that James Guy rented a sloop for 20 days from John Anderson of Pocomock at the rate of 1800 lbs tobacco per month. Sworn before Will. Stevans, 16 May 1677. Presented to the court 19 January 1677/78. (p. 108, 109)

Ambrose White received 40,000 lbs tobacco from John Cole for the sale of a 700 acre plantation (once owned by Nicholas Waddeloe) at Pungoteag. Signed 18 January 1677/78, Amb. White. (p. 109)

The court was to be continued 18 February. Signed, S. Littleton. (p. 109)

Accomack County Court--18 February 1677/78

Present: Maj. Jno. West
         Maj. Edm. Bowman   Capt. Edm. Scarburgh
         Capt. Wm. Custis   Mr. John Drumond (p. 110)

John Jenkins declared that he had sued Robert Atkins, who had killed Jenkins' hog, that had been sold by mistake. Atkins acknowledged the mistake and offered to pay 220 lbs tobacco and the cost of the suit. It was so ordered. (p. 110)

Phillip Quinton was granted a certificate for the next assembly showing that he had been employed by Maj. John West to obtain beef "for the country's service" for 30 days. (p. 110)

Maj. Gen. Jno. Custis entered the court and Maj. West exited. (p. 110)

At the last court Maj. John West had received an attachment against the estate of John Tarr; West proved the debt to be 600 lbs tobacco. The sheriff attached one hogshead of tobacco in the possession of Wm. Blake and 450 lbs tobacco in the possession of James Tayler. Ordered that the debt be satisfied. (p. 110)

Maj. West entered and Maj. Bowman exited for the following action:
Maj. Edm. Bowman was granted a judgment of 314 lbs tobacco against Thomas Goodeing, who was to pay the debt and court costs. (p. 110)

Maj. Jno. West had been granted an attachment of 1537 lbs tobacco against the estate of Wm. Norton. Ordered that the debt and court costs be paid. (p. 110)

Maj. West entered the court. (p. 111)

Thomas Bourows assigned power of attorney to Mr. John Tankard to confess a judgment of 733 lbs tobacco due to John Cole. Signed 18 February 1677/78, Thomas Bourows. Witnesses: Amb. White and Daniel Jenifer.
Mr. John Tankard confessed the above debt, and Thomas Burrowes was ordered to pay the debt and court costs. (p. 111)

Henry Bramal assigned power of attorney to Mr. John Tankard to confess a judgment of 428 lbs tobacco due to John Cole. Signed 18 February

1677/78, Henry (X) Bramal. Witnesses: Richard Hill and Nathaniel Mason.

Mr. John Tankard confessed the above debt, and Henry Bramul was ordered to pay the debt and court costs. (p. 111)

Capt. Custis exited the court. (p. 111)

Nathaniel Bradford sued Daniel Owen for a debt; the court referred the case to Capt. Wm. Custis for examination and final determination. (p. 111)

Accomack County Court--19 February 1677/78

Present: Col. Southy Littleton   Capt. Wm. Custis
    Maj. Edm. Bowman   Mr. Richard Bally (p. 111)

Joice Smith presented the will of John Smith (deceased) in which no executor had been named. At Joice's request, she was granted letters of administration. (side note: "The will whereon this order is grounded is recorded in the book B in folio 86 & 87.") (p. 111, 112)

The difference between Daniel Makarty and Wm. Symons over a year's service had been referred to this court; Makarty had not proved his claim, so the suit was dismissed with Makerty paying court costs. (p. 112)

A certificate for the next assembly was granted to Xopher Thomson, who swore that he and his horse served 14 days during the late rebellion. (p. 112)

Maj. Gen. Jno. Custis entered the court and Col. Littleton exited. (p. 112)

Col. Southy Littleton was granted a judgment of 847 lbs tobacco against John Tayler, who was ordered to pay the debt and court costs. (p. 112)

Col. Littleton entered the court. (p. 112)

Mrs. Tabitha Browne claimed that she had exhibited a petition for a debt due her from the estate of Japhet Cooke. A caveat was entered for her in priority, but she requested administration because most of the debt was in horses which might perish for lack of care. Since administration could not be legally granted until nine months had elapsed, it was ordered that she take the estate into her possession and be responsible for it until further order. (p. 112)

Sara Ebourne came to court and chose as her guardian, Peter Walker, who promised to teach her to read and sew. Ordered that Walker care for the orphan till she reached 16 years of age. (p. 112)

Maj. Gen. Custis and Maj. West exited the court. (p. 113)

Maj. Gen. John Custis sued Maj. Jno. West and Capt. Charles Scarburgh for 7481 lbs tobacco and exhibited a bill to the court. It appeared there was due to Custis 4194 lbs tobacco, so it was ordered that West and Scarburgh pay that sum and court costs. (p. 113)

Maj. West entered the court. (p. 113)

A certificate to the next assembly was granted to Nathan Bougherty who claimed that he had two certificates for five cattle, as sworn by John Clarke. (p. 113)

The suit of Nathanl. Bradford (attorney: Charles Holden) against Daniel Owin for defamation was referred to a jury of which Mr. Wm. Anderson was foreman:
Wm. German	Jon. Owen	Xophr. Thomson
Tho. Hall	Jno. Renny	James Walker
Wm. Nock	Jno. Stokely	George West
Tho. Osburne	Jno. Tayler	

Verdict: After examining the evidence, the jury found no proof of the defamatory words and no proof of damages sustained. Bradford had not claimed any damages except for court costs, which were granted. Signed, Wm. Anderson, Wm. Nock and Chr. Thomson. (p. 113)

Deposition of James Ewell aged about 30 years: Ewell was working at Nathaniel Bradford's when Bradford's people went out hog hunting. They brought home three dead hogs, one of which turned out to be Wm. Burton's hog. Bradford seemed very sorry and said there was no other way but to go and pay him or give him another hog. Signed 18 February 1677/78, James (I) Ewell. (p. 113)

At the request of Peter Walker, it was ordered that he take possession of and care for the estate of Sara Eborne, orphan, in her behalf. He was to be accountable to the court. (p. 114)

19 FEBRUARY 1677/78

Jonathan Owen had procured an attachment of 2110 lbs tobacco against the estate of John Tarr. The sheriff served the attachment against: 450 lbs tobacco and a heifer in the hands of James Tayler, 600 lbs tobacco in the hands of Wm. Blake, 190 lbs tobacco in the hands of John Bowin, and 3000 lbs tobacco and a mare in the hands of Wm. Wyatt. Ordered that the debt and court costs be satisfied. (Side note: The order was satisfied from tobacco in the hands of Jno. Bowin and Wm. Blake, 15 March 1678/79, signed Benj. Eyre.) (p. 114)

Deposition of John Bowin aged about 33 years: John Tarr Sold his plantation to Will. Wayt for 7000 lbs tobacco. Waite delivered a horse, bridle and saddle valued at 2000 and at the next crop two hogsheads of tobacco. The rest was to be paid in two years time. Signed 19 February 1677/78, John (+ with a line above and below) Bowen.

Deposition of Thomas Osburne: The same as above. Signed 19 February 1677/78, Thomas Osburne. (p. 114)

Ralph Justice was granted an attachment of 400 lbs tobacco against the estate of Evan Davis. The attachment was served on "one couch with a hide to back and bottom" and an old chest without a lock. Ordered that the debt and court costs be satisfied. (p. 114)

A certificate to the next assembly was granted to Jno. Clearke, who swore that he had carried 15 gallons of tar aboard the *Admiral* for the King's service. (p. 114)

Mr. Tho. Welburne sued Robt. Bracy but failed to prosecute. A nonsuit was granted against Welburne, who was also to pay court costs. (p. 115)

The suit of Thomas Hall against John Cropper had been referred to this court. There was not a full court, so the jury had found Cropper guilty and left further proceedings to this court. Cropper had fraudulently and purposefully deceived Hall in order to buy Hall's servant, who himself owed Hall 1000 lbs tobacco. Cropper also entertained the servant, which was contrary to law. Ordered that Cropper pay Hall 1000 lbs tobacco (the amount the servant, Richard Price, owed) and 300 lbs tobacco for entertaining Price, along with court costs.

Mr. Robt. Huchinson was foreman of the jury:

Robt. Atkinsom	Wm. Martiall	Henry Reade
Ralph Doe	Barthol. Meares	Jno. Savage
Arthur Frame	Tho. Nixson	Morgan Thomas
Wm. German	Jnoath. Owin	

The jury found Jno. Cropper guilty. Signed, Robt. Huchinson. (p. 115)

Mr. Henry Parke (attorney: Mr. Ed. Ashby) sued Mr. James Matts, whose attorney, Mr. Tankard, requested the case be referred to the next court, which was granted. (p. 115)

James Atkinson confessed owing 720 lbs to Mr. Amb. White. Ordered he pay the debt and court costs. (Side note: Order was executed 14 December 1678, signed Ben. Eyre, subsheriff.) (p. 115)

James Atkinson confessed owing 300 lbs tobacco to John Cole. Ordered that he pay the debt and court costs. (p. 116)

The suit of Capt. Charles Scarburgh and Maj. John West against Capt. Edm. Scarburgh (attorney: Mr. Amb. White) was referred to the next court. (p. 116)

Accomack County Court--20 February 1677/78

Present: Col. Southy Littleton   Capt. Wm. Custis
    Maj. Edm. Bowman   Mr. John Drummond (p. 116)

Barth. Meares' servant girl named Margret Canady was judged to be 14 years old and was ordered to serve accordingly. (p. 116)

Canutus Bence confessed a judgment of 985 lbs tobacco due to John Savage (attorney: Mr. Tankard). Ordered that Bence pay the debt and court costs. (p. 116)

Woodman Stockly failed to appear to answer the complaint of Mary Willson in chancery. Ordered that the sheriff take him into custody for contempt and cause him to appear at the next court. (p. 116)

Thomas Osburne had been granted an attachment of 1162 lbs tobacco against the estate of Peter Pecoe. The sheriff served the attachment on 415 lbs tobacco and 4 1/8 barrels of Indian corn. As 855 lbs tobacco was proved to be due, it was ordered that that sum be paid along with court costs. (p. 116)

Mary Tilghman, executrix of Rich. Tilghman, sued Cornelius Stevens, but she failed to appear to prosecute; the suit was dismissed. (p. 116)

20 FEBRUARY 1677/78

John Cole sued Thomas Cliffen for 377 lbs tobacco, but Cliffen failed to appear. If he did not appear at the next court, the judgment was to pass against the sheriff. (p. 117)

Ambrose White sued Thomas Rogers for 300 lbs tobacco [but Rogers did not appear]. If he did not appear at the next court, the judgment was to pass against the sheriff. (p. 117)

John Cole sued John Newell for a debt, but Newell claimed that Cole did not demand the debt according to law. The suit was dismissed. (p. 117)

John Cole sued Peter Yorke for 304 lbs tobacco, but Yorke failed to appear. If he did not appear at the next court, the judgment was to pass against the sheriff. (p. 117)

John Cole sued Garret Supple for 359 lbs tobacco, but Supple failed to appear. If he did not appear at the next court, the judgment was to pass against the sheriff. (p. 117)

John Cole sued Xopher Sadbury for 715 lbs tobacco, but Sadbury failed to appear. If he did not appear at the next court, the judgment was to pass against the sheriff. (p. 117)

Robt. Holliday sued Thomas Bagwell for a debt, but the court found no cause for action and dismissed the suit. (p. 118)

Maj. John West sued Mr. Amb. White but failed to prosecute; the suit was dismissed. (p. 118)

Mr. Amb. White was granted a judgment of 224 lbs tobacco against Edward Jellson. Ordered that Jellson pay the debt and court costs. (Side note: Served on Edwd. Jellson 14 December 1678.) (p. 118)

John Frankling sued Henry Sellman but failed to appear to prosecute; the suit was dismissed. (p. 118)

John Cole sued Robt. Holliday for a debt, but the court dismissed the suit. (p. 118)

Maj. West and Capt. Hill entered the court. (p. 118)

Thomas Tyer assigned power of attorney to Mr. Ambrose White and/or Mr. Wm. Anderson to represent him in the suit of Mikell Hewit, widow, and confess a judgment of 503 lbs tobacco and court costs. Signed 19 February 1677/78, Tho. (&) Tyer. Witness: Ben. Eyre.

Mr. Amb. White confessed the above judgment to Michol Huit, executrix of Robt. Huit (deceased). (p. 118)

John Cole sued Mr. James Tuck for 2596 lbs tobacco; proclamation was made three times, but Tuck failed to appear. If he did not appear at the next court, judgment was to pass against the sheriff.

Mr. James Tuck came into open court and acknowledged owing Cole 2500 lbs tobacco. Ordered that Tuck pay that sum with court costs. The previous judgment against the sheriff was reversed. (p. 118)

Last night Arthur Frame assaulted Benjamin Aires, a public officer who had been sent by the court to preserve the peace. Frame was taken into the sheriff's custody for "his presumption and contempt." Frame humbly submitted himself and said he was sorry; he did not know that Aires was a public officer. Ordered that he pay court costs and be discharged this time. (p. 119)

William Martiall acknowledged a judgment of 526 lbs tobacco due to Mrs. Tabitha Browne. Ordered that Martiall pay the debt and court costs. (p. 119)

Maj. Bowman exited the court for the following action:
Mr. William Anderson sued Maj. Edm. Bowman, who before the court appealed to the next general court, which was granted. Both parties gave security. (p. 119)

Maj. William Spencer sued Edward Hamond for 926 lbs tobacco, but Hamond failed to appear. If he did not appear at the next court, the judgment was to pass against the sheriff. (p. 119)

John Cole sued John Huchinson, glazier, for 372 lbs tobacco, but the sheriff could not find Huchinson. Ordered that attachment be granted against Huchinson's estate wherever it could be found in the county. (p. 119)

Col. Littleton exited the court for the following action:
Col. Southy Littleton was granted a judgment of 430 lbs tobacco against Richard Williams for surveying Williams' land. Ordered that Williams pay the debt and court costs. (p. 120)

John Watts had been granted an attachment of 605 lbs tobacco against the estate of Evan Davis. The attachment was served on three cattle, one of which was a cow "with a broad horn like a steer." (Side note: Satisfied 14 March 1678/79, signed by Ben Eyre, subsheriff.) (p. 120)

John Cole was granted a judgment of 719 lbs tobacco against John Cropper, who was ordered to pay the debt and court costs. (p. 120)

The suit of John Rainy against William Wallis for a debt was referred to the next court. Cornutus Bence entered himself as security for the appearance of Wallis. (p. 120)

A certificate to the next assembly was granted to William Chace who swore that he served under Capt. Wm. Whittington for 30 days. (p. 120)

The suit of Nathaniel Bradford against James Ewell for a debt was referred to the next court. (p. 120)

The suit of Nathaniel Bradford against James Ewell for trespass was referred to the next court. (p. 120)

Col. Littleton exited the court. (p. 121)

It appeared, according to the verdict of a jury, that John Cropper transported 19 head of cattle from the county contrary to law. Ordered that Cropper pay 19,000 lbs tobacco to Col. Southy Littleton "in behalf of himself and the county" along with court costs.
Cropper requested liberty to appeal to the next general court, which was granted if Cropper put in security by 10 March. If that was done, Littleton was also to put in security.
Mr. Maxamn. Gore was the foreman of the jury:

Wm. Browne	Geo. Nich. Hack	Tobias Selby
Thomas Burros	Bartho. Meares	John Tanner
Wm. Burton	Isaac Metcalfe	James Walker
Ralph Doe	Daniel Owin	

Deposition of Ann Fox aged about 22 years, 21 November 1677: At the order of John Cropper about 19 cattle belonging to the estate of Mrs. Rodia Fausit were conveyed out of the county. Also several things like bedding and household goods were taken away from the plantation by night in the shallop belonging to Maj. Wm. Spencer. Signed, Ann (AF) Fox.

Deposition of Joseph Woodland aged about 18 years: Last March, John Cropper ordered Owen Jackson and John Coulston (Cropper's servant)

to drive 19 cattle into Maryland. If anyone stopped or hindered them, Cropper ordered them to "make what resistance and opposition they could." Cropper himself helped to drive the cattle as far as Daniel Darbie's. Woodland had since seen 18 or the cattle alive in Maryland. Signed 21 February 1677/78, Joseph (u) Woodland.
Verdict of the jury: The defendant was found guilty. Signed 20 February 1677/78, Maxamilian Gore, foreman. (p. 121)

John Franklin sued Henry Sellman but did not appear to prosecute. A nonsuit was granted against Franklin, who was to pay the court costs. (p. 121)

Deposition of Mary Briggs aged about 30 years: At the house of Ralph Doe last summer she heard Doe and John Tanner reckon the accounts between them. Doe admitted that he owed Tanner "five hundred and odd pounds of tobacco." Signed, Mary Brigs.
Deposition of Robert Briggs, 17 January 1677/78: Briggs affirmed the above deposition before S. Littleton. Signed, Robert (R) Briggs and S. Littleton.
John Tanner had petitioned the court for a judgment on an attachment served on the estate of Ralph Doe, but Doe appeared in open court, bailed the attachment, "arrested" Tanner to this court, and produced an account against Tanner. Ordered that both suits be dismissed with each paying their own charges. (p. 122)

In the court held 19 April 1676, Mrs. Anna Boat obtained a judgment of 565 lbs tobacco against William Chace, who was summoned to show why the debt should not be paid. Since he was unable to do so, he was ordered to pay the debt and court costs. (p. 122)

Maj. West exited the court. (p. 122)

Mr. Maxamilln. Gore confessed a judgment of 832 lbs tobacco due to Maj. John West. Ordered that Gore pay the debt and court costs. (p. 122)

Mr. Max. Gore was granted a judgment of 1338 lbs tobacco against John Cropper, who was ordered to pay the debt and court costs. (p. 122)

The suit of Netter Johnson against Ambrose White was dismissed, there being no cause for action. (p. 122)

William Chace confessed a judgment of 680 lbs tobacco due to Maxlln. Gore. It was ordered that he pay the debt and court costs. (Side note:

Wm. Chace paid 30 October 1678. Signed, Ben. Eyre, subsheriff.) (p. 123)

Walter Read sued William Chace but failed to appear to prosecute. Chace was granted a nonsuit against Read, who was to pay court costs. (p. 123)

Tobias Selvy sued John Harmor for 800 lbs tobacco, but Harmor failed to appear. If he did not appear at the next court, the judgment was to pass against the sheriff. (p. 123)

Nathaniel Bradford acknowledged his error: using "bad words and ill language" he did "abuse and miscall Mr. Edward Revell in a very uncivil manner, not at all becoming a civil neighbor." Bradford expressed willingness to pay court charges. Signed 20 February 1677/78, Nathaniel Bradford. (p. 123)

James Prier aged about 28 years declared that he had been sent by his master Maj. West to Watts Island. There John Tayler advised Prier to come to this court, where "if I would meet with him, he warranted me that he would procure me my freedom, and if I would not come, I was a fool." Trusting him, Prier stopped "loading his sloop in pursuance of his promise, in which I find I was and am deceived." Signed 20 February 1677/78, James (S) Pryer. Witness: James Tuck. (p. 123)

Charles Holden petitioned that he had obtained on 16 January 1677/78, a judgment of 900 lbs tobacco and court costs against Jno. Cropper, who according to the sheriff had now moved from the county. Holden requested that Cropper's land be valued and that the debt be paid from the same. Presented to the court 20 February 1677/78, and recorded by Jno. Washbourne. (p. 124)

Accomack County Court--21 February 1677/78

Present: Col. Southy Littleton   Capt. Richd. Hill
          Maj. Jon. West   Mr. Jno. Drummond
          Maj. Edm. Bowman (p. 124)

Mr. William Anderson, attorney of John Anderson, sued James Guy, who failed to appear. An order for 1200 lbs tobacco passed against the sheriff, who returned 1600 lbs tobacco in the hands of Maj. Jno. West and James Rainy. Ordered that the debt be satisfied from that sum. (p. 124)

Nathaniel Bradford "swore profanely" in open court. Ordered that he be fined 50 lbs tobacco and court costs. (p. 124)

James Walker petitioned to be paid for attending court seven days as a witness for Thomas Williams. Ordered that Williams pay Walker 280 lbs tobacco and court costs. (p. 124)

George Charnock petitioned to be paid for attending court five days as a witness for Nathaniel Bradford. Ordered that Bradford pay Charnock 200 lbs tobacco and court costs. (p. 124)

George Charnock, who was summoned as a witness in the suit of Col. Southy Littleton against Jno. Stratton, attended court five days. Since Stratton had agreed to pay all charges arising in the suit, it was ordered that Stratton pay Charnock 200 lbs tobacco and court costs. (p. 124)

A certificate to the next assembly was granted to Henry Custis, who swore that he had not been paid for the 43 days he served on the Bay and at James Town as a lieutenant to Col. Sou. Littleton. Signed, S. Littleton and John West. (p. 125)

Court was adjourned till 16 April 1678. Signed, John Washbourne, court clerk. (p. 125)

Accomack County Court--16 April 1678

Present: Col. Southy Littleton   Capt. William Custis
           Maj. Edm. Bowman   Capt. Richard Hill (p. 125)

Governor Herbert Jeffreys' commission was read in open court: The Governor was required by the King to appoint lower courts of justice in the counties. Eight of the "most judicious, honest persons in the county" were to be appointed, four to eight of which were to be members of the quorum. These persons were to take the oaths of justice of the peace, allegiance and supremacy. For the "better dispatch of all business" it was now thought fit that two persons be added to every commission. The governor expressed confidence in the loyalty, ability and integrity of:

16 APRIL 1678

Col. Southy Littleton, Capt. Charles Scarburgh, Maj. John West, Maj. Edmund Bowman, Mr. John Wise, Capt. Daniell Jenifer and Capt. William Custis--all members of the quorum. Justices of the peace were: Capt. Edmund Scarburgh, Capt. Richard Hill, Mr. Richard Bayly, Mr. Obedience Johnson, Mr. John Wallop and Capt. Hillary Stringer. They were granted power to determine suits, take depositions and inflict punishment. Signed 4 April 1678, Herb. Jeffreys. Recorded 25 April 1678, by Jno. Washbourne, court clerk. (p. 125, 126)

Since Mr. John Wise petitioned to be exempted from public employment because of "age and weakness of body" the Governor gave Wise liberty to hold the office or to be discharged. Signed 3 April 1678, Herb. Jeffreys.

On 16 April 1678, Mr. John Wise presented the Governor's order and accepted the part that allowed him "a writ of ease." Signed, John Wise. (p. 126, 127)

Presentments of the grand jury 16 April 1678:
--John Stokly, for breaking the Sabbath.
--"Breach of Sabbath committed by Ince Owen to William Stokely's wife."
--Seborn Williams, for fornication (presented by John Stratton).
--Ann Bayly, Jr., for fornication.
--Elizabeth Cable, for fornication.
--Frances Chambers, who lived at Maj. West's, for fornication.
--Sarah Furnis, who lived at Maj. West's, for fornication.
--Complaint was made to Thomas Clifton (one of the grand jury) that "one Sabbath day there was very few in the church but at the same time above twenty drinking at Jno. Cole's house the time of sermon."
--Mary Wells, at Mr. Tho. Johnson's, for fornication.
Ordered that the sheriff summon the above persons to the next court to answer their presentments. (p. 127)

Mr. John Bagwell was foreman of the grand jury sworn for the following year:

Mr. Jno. Betts	Mr. Roger Miles	Mr. Stephan Warrington
Mr. Wm. Chace	Mr. Jno. Savage	Mr. Geo. West
Mr. Petr. Clavill	Mr. Jno. Stokely	Mr. Rich. Williams
Mr. Jno. Franklin	Mr. Garrt. Supple	Mr. Thomas Williams
Mr. Wm. Garman	Mr. James Tayler	
Mr. Howell Glading	Mr. Tho. Tayler	
Mr. Tho. Halbe	Mr. Hend. Waggaman	(p. 128)

Elisabeth Truit in open court chose her brother-in-law, Robert Davis, as her guardian. Ordered that John Barnes deliver the orphan's estate to Davis, who was to take care of the orphan and the estate till she came of age. (p. 128)

Maj. Jno. West entered the court. (p. 128)

Steaphen Warrington's servant boy named James Fairfax was judged to be 11 years old and was ordered to serve accordingly. (p. 128)

John Barnes' servant boy named Thomas Duell was judged to be 12 years old and was ordered to serve accordingly. (p. 128)

Capt. Hillary Stringer's servant boy named Benedict Talbot was judged to be 17 years old and was ordered to serve accordingly. (p. 128)

The last will and testament of Robert Mason was proved by the oath of William Nock on 18 February 1677/78, and by Jno. Sturgis on 16 April 1678. (p. 128)

John Collins acknowledged a judgment of 989 lbs tobacco due to Mrs. Tabitha Browne. Ordered that Collins pay the debt and court costs. (p. 128)

The suit of Mr. Henry Parke against Mr. James Matts was referred to the next court. (p. 128)

A certificate to the next assembly was granted to Richard Piwell who swore that he had not been paid for 30 days he spent in the employ of Maj. John West. He had been "getting and killing meat for the country's service." (p. 129)

John Cole was granted a judgment of 104 lbs tobacco and six day's work against Peter Yorke. Ordered that Yorke pay the debt, work and court costs. The former order against the sheriff was dismissed. (p. 129)

Thomas Cliffen confessed a judgment of 307 lbs tobacco due to John Cole. Ordered that Cliffen pay the debt and court costs. The sheriff was acquitted from the order at the last court. (p. 129)

Maj. William Spencer sued Edward Hamond for a debt, but Hamond refused to answer. With the consent of both parties, the case was ordered continued at the next court. (p. 129)

16 APRIL 1678

Garret Supple confessed a judgment of 359 lbs tobacco due to John Cole. Ordered that Supple pay the debt and court costs. The previous order against the sheriff was reversed. (p. 129)

Maj. West exited the court. (p. 129)

The Governor addressed the following to Col. Southy Littleton and the rest of the justices of Accomack County: Thomas Welburne, Gentleman, was appointed to the commission and was to be sworn at the next court. Signed 5 April 1678, Herb. Jeffreys.
Mr. Thomas Welburnes took the oaths of justice of the peace, allegiance and supremacy. (p. 129, 130)

Mr. Jno. Wallop and Mr. Tho. Welburne entered the court. (p. 130)

Nathaniel Bradford had sued James Uell; upon examination of the accounts, it appear that there was only 39 lbs tobacco due, an amount beneath the court's jurisdiction. The suit was dismissed. (p. 130)

Mr. Johnson entered the court and Capt. Hill exited. (p. 130)

An order had passed against the sheriff for the nonappearance of John Hanmer, but since Tobias Selvy also failed to appear to prosecute, the order against the sheriff and the suit were dismissed. (p. 130)

John Prettiman, Wm. Aillworth and other inhabitants of Masongo complained against Tobias Bull for "stopping and fencing the road or Church Path." Ordered that the sheriff summon Bull to the next court. Edward Moore, Jr., George Johnson, Timothy Coe and Jno. Rainy were requested to view the road to see if it was a customary route. They were to determine the most convenient road and report to the next court. (p. 130)

Certificate was granted to Mr. Robert Huchinson for 600 acres for transporting:

Henry Barnes	Ann Dupper	Vincent Oliver
James Chapman	Wm. Flower	Rich. Owen
Jno. Charles	Margret Hill	Joan Thrift
Nich. Dunn	Alice Keyes	Wm. Wale

(p. 130)

Mr. Welburne exited the court. (p. 130)

Mr. Thomas Welburne's servant girl named Elizabeth Poole was judged to be 11 years old and was ordered to serve accordingly. (p. 130)

In the difference between Nathaniel Bradford and James Uell, Bradford had declared for 6000 lbs tobacco and exhibited a bond for the performance of a condition which he claimed was forfeited. Ordered that the case be referred to the next court; Mr. Arthur Upshot and Wm. Nock were to view the alleged damage and report at the next court. (p. 130)

Deposition of Thomas Blake aged about 20 years: On 16 February, Blake was at the house of Xopher Thomson and heard Dick the Indian make a bargain to live with Thomson, who offered to "draw writings if you will, but I think it is needless, for you (speaking to the said Indian) do not understand it." Thomson then told Dick to say the bargain before Blake and Jno. Hornsby, and Thomson repeated it: the Indian was to pay three barrels of Indian corn and 200 lbs tobacco for "meat, drinking, washing and lodging." The Indian answered "that for his washing, he should not trouble himself." Thomson gave the Indian a bottle of brandy and told him to "have a care of his bottle." The Indian said he would return next Tuesday. Signed 16 April 1678, Thomas Blake.

Deposition of Jno. Hornsby aged about 27 years: The above deposition was the truth. Signed 18 April 1678, by Jno. (IH) Jaunsby (sic) before Col. Southy Littleton. (p. 131)

Accomack County Court--17 April 1678

Present: Col. Southy Littleton   Mr. Obedience Johnson
           Maj. Jno. West   Mr. Jno. Wallop (p. 131)

James Atkinson confessed a judgment of 405 lbs tobacco due to Maj. Edm. Bowman. Ordered that Atkinson pay the debt and court costs. (p. 131)

Maj. Bowman entered the court and Col. Littleton exited. (p. 131)

James Gray's servant boy named Jno. Ach was judged to be 13 years old and was ordered to serve accordingly. (p. 131)

Maj. Bowman exited the court and Capt. Custis entered. (p. 131)

Maj. Edmond Bowman sued Howell Glading for 2072 lbs tobacco; the court examined the account and ordered that Glading pay 1400 lbs tobacco and court costs. They desired more proof for the article relating to the rent. (p. 131)

17 APRIL 1678

Thomas Cliffon confessed a judgment of 1200 lbs tobacco due to Maj. Edmond Bowman, administrator of the estate of Jno. Hogben (deceased). Ordered that Cliffon pay the debt and court costs. (Side note: served 14 December 1678, Ben Eyre, subsheriff.) (p. 132)

Col. Littleton and Maj. Boman entered the court. (p. 132)

Bartholemew Meares was granted a judgment of 1000 lbs tobacco against John Cole. Ordered that Cole pay the debt and court costs. (p. 132)

Capt. Hill entered the court. (p. 132)

John Stratton sued Jane Broade for a pot she had broken. Upon examination of the case, the court determined that the pot was broken accidentally and that Stratton had no cause for action. He was to pay court costs. (p. 132)

Maj. Bowman and Maj. West exited the court. (p. 132)

On behalf of himself and Charles and Perry Leatherbury, Maj. Edm. Bowman claimed that Jane Diton, during her time of service, had borne two bastards; this was acknowledged by Diton. It was ordered that she serve Bowman four years on behalf of Charles and Perry Leatherbury and pay court costs. (p. 132)

Deposition of Darkes Aleworth aged about 50 years: A year ago February at Mr. Jno. Stratton's house, "I heard the wench say she was undone." She said she would be hanged, for "I have broken the pot foot." Signed 17 April 1678, Darkas (X) Aleworth.

Deposition of Patience Thornton aged about 17 years: "I did see the wench roll the pot from the quarter house to the great house and took up the foot and fell acrying." Signed Patience (X) Thornton. (p. 132)

Maj. Bowman entered the court. (p. 132)

David Davinson, servant boy to Richard Jones, Jr., was judged to be 17 years old and was ordered to serve accordingly. (p. 132)

John Cole was granted a judgment of 405 lbs tobacco against Jno. Parker, tailor. Ordered that Parker pay the debt and court costs. (p. 132)

An Indian named Arthur (attorney: Charles Holden) complained that Roger Miles had detained his gun. Ordered that Miles deliver the gun "well fixed" to Arthur and pay court costs. (p. 133)

Richard Kellum, Sr., was granted a judgment of 535 lbs tobacco against Peter Dolby according to a condition of a bond. Ordered that Dolby pay the debt and court costs. (p. 133)

Mr. Jnoson exited the court; Mr. Bally entered. (p. 133)

Bartholemew Meares was granted a judgment of 420 lbs tobacco against William Trafford according to a condition of a bond. Ordered that Trafford pay the debt and court costs. (p. 133)

George Charnock was granted a judgment of 400 lbs tobacco against Edward Brotherton for fees and charges incurred during Elizabeth Man's imprisonment. Ordered that Brotherton pay the debt and court costs. (p. 133)

John Watts sued John Best (attorney: Mr. Tankard) for 200 lbs tobacco and for security for two cows and calves, but Watts did not prove his petition. The suit was dismissed with Watts paying court costs. (p. 133)

Thomas Barnet sued Henry Selman for 1340 lbs tobacco, but Selman could not be found by the sheriff. At his petition, Barnet was granted an attachment against the estate of Sellman wherever it could be found in the county.
Henry Sellman came into court and requested to bail the attachment; it was so ordered with Sellman giving bond to answer at the next court. (side note: "Rich. Holland deposition recorded in folio 135.") (p. 133)

Maj. West entered the court. (p. 133)

The suit of Wm. Burton (attorney: Mr. Clayton) against Nathaniel Bradford (attorney: Mr. Tankard) was referred to a jury, of which Mr. Max. Gore was the foreman:

Jno. Bagwell	Barth Meares	Mr. Hen. Read
Jno. Barnes	Rich. Niblet	Mr. Arthur Upshot
Wm. Freeman	Peter Parker	Mr. Steven
Wm. Garman	Rich. Piwell	Warrington

Verdict: According to the evidence, Nathaniel Bradford was found guilty. Signed 16 April 1678, Maximillian Gore, foreman.
Ordered that Bradford pay Burton for unlawfully killing a hog. Since Burton was both the owner and informer, he was to be paid 2000 lbs tobacco and court costs.
Nathaniel Bradford was dissatisfied with the judgment and asked to appeal to the next general court. This was granted, with him giving security.

17 APRIL 1678

Deposition of James Euell aged about 30 years: Euell was working at Bradford's when his people went hog hunting and brought home three hogs, one of which happened to belong to William Burton. Bradford seemed to be very sorry and said he would have to go and pay Burton or give him another. Signed, James (E) Ewell. (Side note: It was about three years since Ewell heard Mr. Bradford speak this.)

Deposition of Samuel Beach aged about 31 years: About 2 years 3 months ago, a sow belonging to Wm. Burton came to Beach's house with two barrows that Beach assumed belonged to Nathaniel Bradford. Two or three days later Beach sent word to Bradford, who came and said he had killed one of the barrows and was looking for the other. Beach said the sow belonged to Burton, but Bradford claimed she was his. The sow had always used the area around Beach's house, but after this, he never saw her again. Signed 16 April 1678, Samuel Beach.

Deposition of Sara Beech aged about 36 years: Sara said that her husband had told the truth. Signed 16 April 1678, Sara (0) Beech.

Deposition of Daniel Owin aged about 40 years: After Owin heard a gunshot, he heard Nathaniel Bradford ask if the barrow were dead. Thomas Williams answered that it was a sow. Owin saw Bradford and Williams stand by the dead sow, which Owin knew had belonged to William Burton two years ago Christmas. Signed 16 April 1678, Daniel (O) Owin.

Deposition of Barbery Owen aged about 30 years: "I was in Nickowansin a getting of walnuts. I saw a sow of William Burton's that we let out of our one pen about three or four days ago, and going along, I heard a gun something nigh to me, and presently the sow reeled and fell down, and seeing Thomas Williams come out of the thicket and set his foot upon the sow and stuck her with his knife. Nathaniel Bradford calling to him, asked if the barrow was dead. He answered, it was a sow. My husband being a little space before me, I beckoned to him, and he came back and I told my husband what happened." Signed 16 April 1678, Barbery (H) Owen.

Deposition of Jno. Reeves aged about 28 years: Reeves saw three hogs lying in Nathanl. Bradford's yard; one of them was white. Reeves saw James Euell pulling the bristles off the hogs, but did not know to whom they belonged. Signed 16 April 1678, Jno. Reves. (p. 134, 135)

Deposition of Richd. Holland aged about 43: In April 1677, Mary Holden, wife of Jno. Holden, came to Holland's house and asked for Tho. Barnet, who worked for Holland at that time. Mary asked if Barnet had a cow or not, and Holland replied that he thought he was to get one of the cows that Hen. Selman earned from Capt. Edm. Scarburgh when [Sellman] was with Barnet. Mary asked Holland to ask Barnet if John

Holden should have the cow or not. Finding only Sellman at home, Holland questioned him. Barnet had no cow there; Sellman said that he once offered Barnet 200 lbs tobacco for his share of a cow to be had from Scarburgh, but now he "would not give anything but what the said Barnet could recover by law." Signed 17 April 1678, Rich. (H) Holland. (p. 135)

Arthur Robins, who claimed that the estate of Jno. Hanson (deceased) owed him 30,000 lbs tobacco, requested administration as the greatest creditor. The court found no warrant to grant administration to the greatest creditor, but for the improvement of the estate, granted Robins the power as trustee to sue for debts belonging to Hanson's estate. Robins gave security and was ordered to give an account of the estate. (p. 136)

Arthur Robins had been granted the administration of the estate of William Eborne (deceased) on behalf of the orphans. Several people had since been granted the care of the orphans, and upon their petition had been granted orders to take the orphans' share of the estate. Ordered that they give a yearly account to the orphans' court and give bond with security to be responsible to deliver the estate to the orphans when they came of age. Ordered that Robins deliver no part of the estate till receiving a certificate from the court clerk stating that the guardian had posted bond. (p. 136)

Peter Dolby confessed a judgment of 488 lbs tobacco due to William Spencer (attorney: Mr. Tankard). Ordered that Dolby pay the debt and court costs. (p. 136)

Peter Dolby confessed a judgment of 584 lbs tobacco due to Henry Mathews (attorney: Mr. Tankard). Ordered that Dolby pay the debt and court costs. (p. 136)

Nathaniel Bradford (attorneys: Mr. Tankard and Ch. Holden) sued William Burton for defamation. After examining the case, the court determined that the words spoken were not actionable. A nonsuit was ordered against Nathaniel Bradford, who was to pay court costs. (p. 136)

William Burton sued Nathaniel Bradford for defamation, but the court determined that the defamatory words charged in the petition were not actionable. A nonsuit was ordered against Burton, who was to pay court costs. (p. 136)

17 APRIL 1678

William White was granted a judgment of 525 lbs tobacco against Mr. James Matts, who was ordered to pay the debt and court costs. (p. 137)

Deposition of James Lecat aged about 34 or 35 years: Lecat came to William Freeman's house to witness the division of land between Freeman and Richard Williams. When Col. Littleton came to do it, Freeman's wife told him it should not be done because Mr. Ambr. White was not there, and neither was her husband. However, she had sent for her brother, Richard Williams, and her mother to have the land divided as they had agreed with Littleton. Signed 16 April 1678, John Lecatt. (p. 137)

Richard Williams was granted a judgment of 263 lbs tobacco against William Freeman, who was ordered to pay the debt and court costs. (p. 137)

[Here the deposition of John Lecatt was repeated.]

Upon the petition of Wm. Burton, it was ordered that the sheriff immediately take Nathaniel Bradford into custody till he gave security to be on his good behavior and that he pay court costs. (p. 137)

Upon the petition of Nathaniel Bradford, it was ordered that the sheriff immediately take Wm. Burton into custody till he gave security to be on his good behavior and that he pay court costs. (p. 137)

The suit of William Freeman against John Betts and Elizabeth his wife was dismissed with Freeman paying court costs. (p. 138)

Deposition of Jno. Lecat aged about 34 or 35 years: At William Freeman's house, Lecat heard Freeman's mother-in-law demand from Freeman's wife a gun she had lent Freeman. When Freeman's wife refused, "her mother told her she would have it, and thereupon took it and delivered it to Richard Williams." Signed 17 April 1678, Jno. Lecat. (p. 138)

Accomack County Court--18 April 1678

Present: Maj. Edm. Bowman   Mr. Obedience Johnson
           Capt. William Custis   Mr. Jno. Wallop
           Mr. Richard Bally (p. 138)

John Tankard sued James Ewell for a debt, but Ewell asked to produce further proof at the next court, which was granted. (p. 138)

John Cole sued William Silverthorne for 1122 lbs tobacco, but Silverthorne failed to appear to answer. If he did not appear at the next court, then judgment would pass against the sheriff for the debt and court costs. (p. 138)

Walter Read sued William Chace but did not file his petition according to law. A nonsuit was granted against Read, who also paid court costs. (p. 138)

Sebastian Gingee, attorney of Mrs. Joan Gingee, who was the administratress of Wm. Gingee (deceased), summoned Hend. Waggaman to court upon a scire facias to revive a judgment obtained 18 February 1675. Waggaman showed cause to the contrary, so the suit was dismissed. (p. 138)

Capt. Charles Scarburgh and Maj. John West sued Capt. Edmd. Scarburgh (attorney: Mr. Amb. White). At White's request and with West's consent, the suit was referred to the next court. (p. 138)

Col. Littleton entered the court. (p. 139)

Maj. John West had obtained an attachment of 1500 lbs tobacco against the estate of John Anderson, and West now petitioned that attachment be served "in the hands of Capt. Daniel Jenifer" on 1200 lbs tobacco which was returned. The court granted a judgment of 995 lbs tobacco and court costs on the estate of Anderson in the hands of Jenifer. West also produced a bill for 400 lbs tobacco due to Mr. James Renny from Anderson, but not having proved his bill, the case was referred to the next court. (p. 139)

James Renny assigned power of attorney to Maj. Jno. West to sue and receive debts from anyone in Virginia or Maryland. Signed 3 August 1677, James Rainy. Witnesses: Ed. Brotherton and Hannah (U) Clifton. Presented to the court 18 April 1678, by Maj. West and ordered recorded. (p. 139)

Sebastian Gingee, attorney of Mrs. Joane Gingee, administratress of Mr. William Gingee (deceased), sued Mrs. Anna Bote upon a scire facias to revive a judgment of 3238 lbs tobacco given 18 February 1675. Mr. Geo. Nich. Hack, in behalf of his mother [Mrs. Bote], exhibited an account against Gingee. The court determined that Bote owed 658 lbs tobacco and court costs, which she was ordered to pay. (p. 139)

Col. Littleton exited the court for the following action:
Col. Southy Littleton and Capt. Sebastian Gingee consented to join issue on an account exhibited by Littleton in which Sebastian's father, Capt. Wm. Gingee, owed Littleton 1685 lbs tobacco. Sebastian confessed a judgment or 203 lbs tobacco and 16 pounds sterling along with 712 lbs tobacco if Littleton proved it to be due at the next court. (p. 140)

Mr. Welburne exited the court for the following action:
Mr. Thomas Welburne started an action against Mr. James Matts declaring that he had obtained an order against John Davis for 1050 lbs tobacco and court costs. Davis made his crop last year at Matts' house, but Matts refused to share it. Ordered that Matts, at the next court, give an account of the crop made by Davis and his wife. Matts was also to produce the covenant that was in the possession of John Davis. (p. 140)

Capt. Sebastian Gingee, attorney of Joane Gingee, who was the administratress of William Gingee, was ordered to give security to pay all damages accruing from suits in which he was plaintiff and to cover all just debts contracted in the county by William Gingee. Sebastian and William Anderson presented themselves as security, and the court accepted. (p. 140)

Mr. William Anderson brought Elizabeth Smith's servant boy named Samuel Fittiman to court; Samuel was judged to be 18 years old and was ordered to serve accordingly. (p. 140)

Thomas Osburne was ordered by the court to pack and ship three hogsheads tobacco belonging to Peter Peco. Osburn gave an account of the three hogsheads to the court, which ordered that he be paid 285 lbs tobacco for "his pains in stripping, packing and finding hogsheads and transporting the same to Jno. Ramey's." (p. 140)

The Governor ordered that Capt. Daniell Jenifer be continued as high sheriff of Accomack County; he was to take the oath of high sheriff at the next court. Signed 3 April 1678, Herb. Jeffreys. Presented to the court 18 April 1678, by Capt. Danl. Jenifer.
Capt. Daniel Jenifer was sworn as high sheriff for the ensuing year.
Benjamin Aires was chosen by Capt. Jenifer as the undersheriff and was sworn. (p. 141)

Upon the oath of Mr. James Matts, it was ordered that the sheriff take Charles Wyer into custody till posting bond to keep the peace to all, but especially to Matts. Signed 18 April 1678, S. Littleton. (p. 141)

Peter Parker recorded his ear mark for cattle and his brand, PP. Recorded 25 April 1678, by Jno. Washbourne, court clerk. (p. 141)

Mr. Phillip Fisher recorded his ear mark for cattle. Recorded 25 April 1678, by Jno. Washbourne, court clerk. (p. 141)

Accomack County Court--16 May 1678

Present: Maj. Gen. Jno. Custis
Col. Southy Littleton   Capt. Edmd. Scarburgh
Maj. Edmd. Bowman   Mr. Jno. Wallop (p. 142)

William Crabb (attorney: Mr. Pilsworth) sued Robert Richardson for a debt that Richardson claimed he had paid. Richardson requested till the next court to prove it, which was granted. (p. 142)

Joseph Jackeil, mate to James Senior, the master of *Grossers Adventure*, died in this county and left an estate behind. Since the county court was empowered to take charge of estates of persons dying intestate, the sheriff was ordered to take Jackeil's estate, except for tobacco, and sell it at auction. The sheriff was to give an account at the next court.

Peter Pritchet made it appear to the court that the estate of Joseph Jackeill (deceased) owed him 1300 lbs tobacco for accommodation at his house and for funeral charges. Since Mr. John Wallop admitted owing 2500 lbs tobacco to the estate, it was ordered that Prichard have 1300 lbs tobacco out of Wallop's debt.

Mr. Jno. Wallop admitted owing the estate of Joseph Jackeil (deceased) 2500 lbs tobacco, which he was ordered to pay.

Upon Mr. Henry Parke's petition, it was ordered that a caveat be entered against the estate of Joseph Jackeill (deceased) for 400 lbs tobacco for preaching a funeral sermon. (p. 142)

James Senior, master of the ketch *Grossers Adventure* (consigned to Mr. Thomas Welburne), died intestate and left an estate behind. Welburne requested the court's directions for disposing of the estate. Ordered that Welburne take possession of the tobacco he had left and give an account of it to the next court after giving security. He would be responsible to the court next year. The sheriff was to take the other part of the estate, sell it at auction and give an account at the next court. (p. 143)

A certificate to the next general assembly was granted to Walter Tayler, who swore that he had not been paid for the 28 days that he served the country during the late rebellion. (p. 143)

William Whright presented a certificate signed by Mr. Jno. Wallop proving that he had captured John Watts' runaway servant named Joseph Holliday, who at the time was about 12 miles away from his master's house. (p. 143)

Arthur Upshot and Wm. Nock had been ordered to view the damages on Nathaniel Bradford's plantation where James Ewell recently lived. They found that Ewell had removed 18 apple trees that had been "planted out at a distance." The "dwelling house [was] double covered, but the chimney and gable end of the house [were] damnified" as was a small shed at the end of the house. Signed Arthur (A) Upshot and Wm. Nock.
The suit of Nathaniel Bradford against James Ewell had been referred to this court. Arthur Upshot and Wm. Nock presented their report, and the court ordered that Ewell pay court costs and 280 lbs tobacco for damages suffered by Bradford. (p. 143)

Mr. Henry Parke (attorney: Mr. Tho. Clayton) sued Mr. James Matts (attorney: Mr. Jno. Tankard). Ordered that Matts pay court costs and 200 lbs tobacco, the sum due "for his marriage, as being married with a license." (p. 144)

Deposition of Mary Holden aged about 49 years: A year ago last fall, Thomas Barnet came to Mary's house and asked her to spare one of her sons to assist him in his crop; Barnet was behind in harvest because Henry Sellman had gone to work for Capt. Edmond Scarburgh for cows and calves. Mary spared her son John Rogers for one whole month and several other times "to worm and succor and house the crop." Barnet had sufficiently paid Mary. Signed 16 May 1678, Mary Holden.
It appeared to the court that Henry Sellman owed Thomas Barnet (attorney: Mr. Edwd. Ashby) 20 shillings sterling and 75 lbs tobacco. Ordered that Sellman pay the debt and court costs. (Side note: It was noted that the deposition of Rich. Holand was recorded on p. 135 in the record book [p. 102 of this volume].) (p. 144)

At the last court James Matts was ordered to give an account of Jno. Davis's tobacco in his possession; he did this and it appeared that 232 lbs tobacco was due. Matts was ordered to pay Thomas Welburne that sum and court costs. (p. 144)

Maj. Gen. Jno. Custis exited the court and Maj. West entered. (p. 144)

The suit of John Cole against William Silverthorne was dismissed and last court's order against the sheriff was reversed. (p. 144)

Mr. John Tankard exhibited a bill against Richard Southern (attorney: Mr. Amb. White). The case was referred to the next court. (p. 145)

At the request of James Ewell, the suit of Nathaniel Bradford against Ewell for 1108 lbs tobacco was referred to the next court. (p. 145)

Nathaniel Bradford was granted a judgment of 5000 lbs tobacco against James Ewell, who was ordered to pay the debt and court costs. (p. 145)
James Ewell requested and received an injunction to stop proceedings on the above order until a hearing at the next court. (p. 145)

Arthur Robins, trustee for the estate of Mr. John Hanson (deceased), sued Sebastian Gingee, attorney of Mrs. Joan Gingee, administratress of Capt. Wm. Gingee (deceased). Robins had not shown cause why the judgment should be revived, so it was ordered that the suit be dismissed. (p. 145)

Mr. John Tankard was granted a judgment of 200 lbs tobacco against James Ewell, who was ordered to pay the debt and court costs. Examined in open court by Sou. Littleton. (p. 145)

Accomack County Court--17 May 1678

Present: Col. Southy Littleton
Maj. Edm. Bowman   Mr. Obed. Johnson
Capt. William Custis   Mr. Jno. Wallop (p. 145)

George Charnock confessed a judgment of 585 lbs tobacco due to Charles Holden. Ordered that Charnock pay the debt and court costs. (p. 145)

17 MAY 1678

John Hanning assigned power of attorney to Mr. John Tankard to confess a judgment of 774 lbs tobacco due to John Cole. Signed 16 May 1678, John Hanning. Witnesses: Ben Eyre and Rich. Richards.
Mr. John Tankard confessed the above judgment; ordered that Hanning pay the debt and court costs. (p. 146)

Thomas Besent assigned power of attorney to Mr. John Tankard to confess a judgment of 778 lbs tobacco due to John Cole. Signed 16 May 1678, John Hanning. Witness: John Stokely.
Mr. John Tankard confessed the above judgment, and though he produced a warrant of attorney, he did not prove it. Ordered that if Besent did not pay the debt by next 10 October, then Tankard would have to pay the debt with court costs. (p. 146)

Capt. Edmd. Scarburgh entered the court. (p. 146)
Richard Richards confessed a judgment of 367 lbs due to Jno. Cole. Ordered that Richards pay the debt and court costs. (p. 146)

The suit of Howel Glading against Tobias Bull over a gun was referred to the next court at Bull's request. (p. 146)

Ordered that the inhabitants of the county bring in their lists of tithables to the following individuals:
--Below Occahannock and Edward Hamond's on the Bay Side, to Mr. Obedience Johnson
--Occahannock to Mr. Revell's Bridge on the Bay Side, to Mr. Richard Bally
--From Edward Hamond's Branch to Jno. Cole's on the Sea Side, to Capt. Wm. Custis
--From John Cole's to Gargaphia on the Bay Side, to Maj. Edmd. Bowman
--From Mr. Revell's Bridge to Deep Creek on the Bay Side, to Capt. Charles Scarburgh
--From Deep Creek to Muddy Creek on the Bay Side, to Capt. Richard Hill
--From Muddy Creek on the Bay Side and Gargaphia on the Sea Side up to the uppermost precincts of the county, to Mr. Jno. Wallop. (p. 147)

Will. Spencer assigned power of attorney to John Tankard. Signed, Will. Spencer. Witnesses: Henrery (sic) Stott and Wm. Williams. (p. 147)

Edward Hamond confessed a judgment of 420 lbs tobacco due to Maj. William Spencer. Ordered that he pay the debt and court costs. The former order against the sheriff was reversed. (p. 147)

Maj. West entered the court. (p. 148)

John Fauset entered an action against Rodeah Fawset, executrix of John Fawset (deceased), but she could not be found in the county. At the petition of John Fawset, he was granted an attachment of 5000 lbs tobacco against the estate of Rodiah Fawset where it could be found in the county. (p. 148)

Jno. Watts assigned power of attorney to Mr. Tho. Clayton to act for him in his difference with John Best, surgeon, or any other person. Signed 4 April 1678, Jno. (X) Watts. Witnesses: Daniel Jenifer and Ben. Eyre. (p. 148)

Mr. Welburne entered the court. (p. 148)

The suit of John Watts, planter, against John Best, in an action of covenant, was referred to the next court.
Deposition of Will Aleworth aged about 50 years: While working at the house of Jno. Wats around Shrovetide in 1677, Aleworth heard the people say that they wondered where the doctor was and why he did not come. Even though he had been there six weeks, constantly working at the house, Aleworth had never seen the doctor. And he had been looking for him; Aleworth was lame and wanted to consult the doctor himself. Signed 17 May 1678, Wm. Ailworth.
The suit of Jno. Best against John Watts (attorney: Mr. Jno. Tankard) was referred to the next court. (p. 148)

In the suit of James Matts against Charles Wyer, it was ordered that Wyer return to Matts' service for ten days and find security for the payment of 926 lbs tobacco, or else serve his master for payment of charges and court costs expended in recapturing Wyer. (p. 148)

Mr. Johnson exited the court; Maj. Gen. Jno. Custis entered. (p. 149)

Edward Revell, attorney of Phillip Hanger and Thomas Cock, in behalf of Mr. John Walter and Company, (attorney for the plaintiffs: Mr. Tho. Clayton) summoned Mr. Obedience Johnson, who had written a note to Thomas Cocks saying that Peter Browne's credit was good. However, Peter Brown left the county without paying his debts. It appeared that

17 MAY 1678

Brown had signed a bill binding himself to pay Mr. Walters and Company 905 lbs tobacco. Ordered that Mr. Obedience Johnson pay the debt and court costs. (p. 149)

Deposition of John Savedg aged about 37 years: Obedience Johnson rebuked Tho. Cock for bothering him about a debt Brown owed Cock. Cock said he did not intend to bother Johnson. Rather than being brought to court again, Cock said he "would pay the half of it." Cock then added, "Nay, before you shall be troubled any more about this debt, I will pay the whole myself." Signed 17 May 1678, Jno. (IS) Savadge. (p. 149)

Deposition of Robt. Watson aged about 54 years: About Shrove Tuesday 1677, Watson was at the house of Jno. Watts, who asked if Watson had seen Dr. Best, but Watson had not. When Watson returned, Watts again asked about the doctor and said, "Pray, if you see him, ask him what he mindeth to do, to leave his patient so long in such a sad condition." When Watson was at Pungeteag Church, he purposely went to Mr. Bradford's where he met Dr. Best and "asked him if he had quite given over his patient in so sad a condition. The doctor replied that he must be fluxed [purged]." Watson went on to tell the doctor that "[I am] troubled with the foul disease...and hath been thus twenty years." Signed 17 May 1678, Robt. Watson. (p. 149)

Maj. Bowman exited the court. (p. 149)

Sebast. Gingee, attorney of Mrs. Joan Gingee, the administratress of Capt. Wm. Gingee (deceased), (attorney for the plaintiffs: Mr. Clayton) declared against Maj. Edmd. Bowman for 1744 lbs tobacco--a debt of Hend. Wagaman's for which Gingee had obtained a judgment and execution. Maj. Bowman, then the sheriff, served the execution on Wagaman, and it appeared by the testimonies of Capt. Daniel Jenifer and Mr. Robt. Huchinson that Capt. Gingee had ordered the sheriff to release Waggaman. Ordered that the suit be dismissed with Gingee paying court costs.

Deposition of Robert Huchinson aged about 47 years: About two years ago in March, Capt. Wm. Gingee caused the sheriff, then Maj. Edm. Bowman, to collect a debt from Henrick Wagaman. Bowman "was brought to my house, where the said Capt. Gingee was." After some words, Gingee asked Huchinson to draw a discharge to release Wagaman from the debt, which Huchinson refused to do, saying that Gingee would be in danger of losing his debt. It was concluded that the sheriff should proceed to summon appraisers. Wagaman said he "would tender his estate to release his body," but since he did not have enough to satisfy the debt, Wagaman promised to give security to Gingee. Though warned of the danger by Huchinson, Gingee, upon the promise of Wagaman to pay the debt and charges in six weeks, declared to the sheriff that he wanted Wagaman discharged. Gingee promised Maj. Bowman that he would pay any fees due for the execution, and then Bowman gave Henrick Wagaman his liberty. Signed 17 May 1678, Robt. Hutchinson.

Deposition of Daniel Jenifer aged about 41 years, 17 May 1678: About two years ago last March at Mr. Robt. Huchinson's house in Pungoteeg, Maj. Edmd. Bowman (the sheriff) had Hendrick Wagaman in custody at the suit of Capt. Wm. Gingee. After much discussion, Gingee declared that he wanted Wagaman released from prison. Gingee said he would pay the fees due, and by his order, the sheriff discharged Hendrick Wagaman from prison. Signed 17 May 1678, Daniel Jenifer.

Maj. Edm. Bowman made it appear to the court that he had paid 1119 lbs tobacco to Sebastn. Gingee, attorney of Mrs. Joan Gingee, administratress of Capt. Wm. Gingee (deceased), as partial payment for a servant named Grace Carter. In open court, Bowman relinquished all right to the servant and acquitted Gingee of the same. Ordered that Sebast. Gingee, attorney of Mrs. Joan Gingee, pay the above sum and court costs. (p. 149, 150)

A certificate to the next assembly was granted to Jno. Cole, who presented an account for 288 lbs tobacco delivered by Maj. Gen. Jno. Custis at two different times to the Indians when they brought in their tribute--16 gallons of cider at 18 lbs per gallon. (p. 151)

Daniel Harcort assigned power of attorney to Mr. Tho. Clayton, who was to represent him at the suit of Mrs. Tabitha Browne. Signed 4 May 1678, Daniel (H) Harrot (sic). Witnesses: Sa. Cooper and Ben Eyre. (p. 151)

Maj. Gen. Custis exited the court. (p. 151)

Daniel Harrot confessed a judgment of 400 lbs tobacco due to Mrs. Tabitha Browne, who promised that execution would not issue till the next 10 October. Ordered that Harrot then pay the debt and court costs. (p. 151)

Mr. Bally entered the court. (p. 151)

William Silverthorne sued Hendrick Wagaman for defamation. Mr. Jno. Tankard entered himself security for Wagaman's appearance at the next court, so the case was referred till then.

17 MAY 1678

Deposition of Robt. Huchinson aged about 47 years: On 23 November, William Silverthorne and Stephen Filby were at Huchinson's house at Pungotege when Henrick Wagaman came. They started talking about hogs and hog stealing; Wagaman said Mr. Charles Scarburgh had twice met Silverthorne with Scarburgh's hogs on his back. Scarburgh said, "This is twice I have ketcht you stealing my hogs, but beware the third time." Silverthorne asked Wagaman, "Who said so?" Wagaman replied, "Question me when you will, and I will produce my author," but when Silverthorne again demanded who it was, Wagaman refused to tell him. Signed 17 May 1678, Robt. Huchinson.

Deposition of Stephen Filby aged about 29 years: Robt. Huchinson told the truth, to the best of Filby's knowledge. Signed 17 May 1678, Stephen Philbie. (p. 151)

A certificate was granted to John Aires, who swore that he had received no payment; he, with his boat, was in the country's service for 30 days over the bay at James Town. (p. 151)

Mr. Samuel Sandford was granted a judgment of 641 lbs tobacco against Nicholas Millechop. Ordered that Millechop pay the debt and court costs. (side note: Execution was served on the body of Nich. Millechop, 14 December 1678. Signed, Ben Eyre, subsheriff.) (p. 152)

Deposition of John Rainy aged 40 years or more: Rainy affirmed that on 30 June 1677, he was a witness to a condition and contract between Samll. Cooper and Nicholas Melicchop for building a house on the land of Jno. Evans. However the house was built only by Mellychop. Signed 16 May 1678, Jno. Rainy. (p. 152)

John Barnet confessed a judgment of 602 lbs tobacco due to Max. Gore. Ordered that Barnet pay the debt and court costs. (Side note: Executed on the body of Jno. Barnet on 30 December 1678, by Ben. Eyr, subsheriff.) (p. 152)

Rebecca Holliwell (attorney: Mr. Clayton) sued Jno. Legeat, but he failed to appear to answer the suit. Ordered that if he failed to appear at the next court, then judgment and court costs would pass against the sheriff.

Rebecca Holliwell swore in open court that she was expecting Jno. Legeat's bastard child. Ordered that the sheriff take him into custody till he posted a bond to save the parish from supporting the child. He was also to pay court costs. (p. 152)

Stephen Phillby petitioned for payment for being summoned as a witness and attending court for eight days during Wm. Silverthorne's suit against Hend. Wagaman. Ordered that Silverthorne pay 320 lbs tobacco and court costs. (p. 152)

Mr. Robt. Huchinson petitioned for payment for being summoned as a witness and attending court for eight days during Wm. Silverthorne's suit against Hend. Wagaman. Ordered that Silverthorne pay 320 lbs tobacco and court costs. (p. 152)

Capt. Wm. Custis claimed that Jno. Barnes obliged himself to be charged 500 lbs tobacco for the surveying of 300 acres. Custis produced an obligation signed by Barnes on 16 May 1672. Ordered that Barnes pay the debt and court costs. (p. 152)

Deposition of Wm. Wallis aged about 30 years: Wallis was in the company of Mr. Samll. Sandford when he arrived at the houses where Mr. Samll. Cooper stored Sandford's goods. Wallis was alone with Sandford for some days and affirmed that Sandford positively refused to dispose of any of the goods found in the houses, but instead took care to preserve them "weighing and measuring all and every the said goods before witnesses." Signed 17 May 1678, William (W) Wallis. (p. 153)

Accomack County Court--18 May 1678

Present: Col. Southy Littleton   Capt. Wm. Custis
             Maj. Jno. West   Mr. Richard Bally
     Maj. Edmd. Bowman   Mr. Thomas Welburne (p. 153)

An act of the assembly enjoined the justices to meet in May and November to set the rates of liquors; this the court did on 20 November 1677. Ordered that all "ordinary keepers" proceed according to that order. (p. 153)

Mr. Samll. Sandford sued Samll. Cooper and claimed that he, expecting profit, sent Cooper into this country and entrusted him with a cargo of goods amounting to 347 pounds 3 shillings and 1 penny sterling. Sandford petitioned that Cooper be compelled to give an account of the whole cargo and the proceeds. Ordered that Cooper give an account under oath at the next court; Sandford was to allow him use of all the books necessary. If a dispute arose, it was ordered that Mr. Robt.

Huchinson, Mr. Jno. Welburne, Mr. Wm. Anderson and John Washbourne or any two of them audit the accounts and report to the next court. (p. 153)

Deposition of Ben. Eyre aged about 29 years: At Pokeamoke, Eyre was ordered by Samuel Sandford "to arrest Samuel Cooper to this court." Because Cooper had no security to post for his appearance, Sandford requested him to take all his books and papers to Gargaphia, where he could recollect his memory and prepare a more complete account of his proceedings in Sandford's business. Cooper replied that he could not give a better account that what he and Mr. Hopkins had done. Signed 18 May 1678, Ben. Eyre.

Deposition of Samll. Hopkins aged 42 years: Shortly after arriving in Pocomoke, Mr. Samll. Sandford, requested Hopkins to make an exact account of the goods remaining unsold in his storehouses. Hopkins did this in the presence of several witnesses. Sandford was careful to preserve the goods and positively refused to have anything sold until Mr. Cooper returned to deliver them. Signed 18 May 1678, Samll. Hopkins. (p. 153, 154)

Thomas Barnet and William Chace owed to Richard Holland (attorney: Wm. Steavens) 3000 lbs tobacco by a bond dated 19 December 1677. Ordered that Barnet and/or Chace pay the debt and court costs. (p. 154)

Mr. Welburne exited the court for the following action:
Arthur Robins, trustee for the estate of John Hanson (deceased), petitioned that Mr. Jonathan Waterland owed the estate 16 hogsheads of tobacco. Mr. Thomas Welburne and Mr. Wm. Anderson presented themselves as security for Waterland, who was to give a full account of the estate in his possession by the end of January. Waterland was to be answerable for the just claims due to Hanson's estate. (p. 154)

Mr. Samuel Sandford entered action against Francis Gunby for 602 lbs tobacco, but Gunby could not be found. Sandford was granted an attachment against Gunby's estate for the debt and court costs where it could be found in the county. (p. 154)

Thomas Goodeing exhibited a bill in chancery against Charles Leatherbury, who was granted the liberty of answering at the next court. (p. 155)

Thomas Barnet (attorney: Mr. Ashby) had been granted an attachment against the estate of John Newell; the sheriff returned the attachment served on an 8 or 9 year-old gray mare marked on the buttock with DI, her black colt, and an iron pot. As Newell owed Barnet 1874 lbs tobacco, it was ordered that the judgment and court costs issue on the horses and pot. (Marginal note: executed on a mare and colt appraised at 1100 lbs tobacco, 31 May 1679, signed Ben Eyre, subsheriff.) (p. 155)

Deposition of Jno. Rowles aged about 36 years, sworn before Col. Southy Littleton 15 April 1678: Rowles assigned to Thom. Barnet, two bills of Jno. Newell, who recently lived in the county. Rowles had never received payment for any part--only Barnet had. Signed, John Rowles and S. Littleton. (p. 155)

Maj. West exited the court, and Mr. Bally entered. (p. 155)

Jno. Anderson was given till this court to show why Maj. Jno. West should not be paid 935 lbs tobacco. But since Anderson failed to do so, West consented to suspend the execution till the next court. (p. 155)

The suit of Capt. Charles Scarburgh and Maj. John West against Capt. Edmond Scarburgh was continued to the next court. (p. 155)

William Anderson was granted a judgment of 235 lbs tobacco against Thomas Nixson, who was ordered to pay the debt and court costs. (p. 155)

Deposition of Ben Eyre aged about 29 years: Eyre received from Mr. Edward Southerne, who lived at "the Whorekill", a bill for a debt due to Southerne from Thomas Nixson. Southerne had endorsed the back. Signed Ben Eyre and sworn in open court 18 May 1678.

Deposition of Thomas Bagwell aged about 36 years, 18 May 1678: About the beginning of May, Bagwell was at "the horekeal" at Ed. Southern's house, when Wm. Burton presented Southerne with a receipt written by Capt. Wm. Custis for tobacco that Custis had paid Southerne by the way of Mr. Avery. After Southerne read the receipt, he refused to sign it because he had requested the bill Capt. Custis paid to Wm. Anderson; Southerne said he must pay Mr. Every (sic) again and acknowledged that if Tho. Nixson paid the tobacco to Custis or George Johnson, it would be acceptable. Signed, Tho. Bagwell.

Deposition of Samll. Hopkins aged 42 years: As far as Hopkins knew, Mr. Wm. Anderson had no accounts in Mr. Samll. Cooper's book that he kept for the sale of Mr. Sandford's goods. However, Cooper verbally directed Hopkins to charge Mr. Nubold's debts to Mr. Anderson. The error was later found and "corrected, as many other errors were, which were found in the said Mr. Cooper's accounts." Hopkins knew of no person paying anything on Mr. Anderson's account. Signed 18 May 1678, Samll. Hopkins.

Deposition of Sa. Cooper: A hogshead of tobacco was paid on the account of Mr. Tho. Newbold to Mr. Wm. Anderson by Cooper by the order of Mr. Samll. Sandford. Certain persons had given Newbold credit by charging their own accounts. The hogshead of tobacco charged to Mr. Newbold was not obliterated by Cooper's order. Signed 18 May 1678, Sa. Cooper. (p. 156)

Thomas Edge had misdemeaned himself in the presence of the court and was ordered taken into custody till finding security to build a pair of stocks by the next court. Because James Euell had presented himself as security for Edge, it was ordered that Ewell build or cause to be built a new pair of stocks at the court house between this court and the next, or pay 400 lbs tobacco and court charges. (p. 157)

[The following entry was recorded in Latin:]
Joanna Gingee, widow of William Gingee, and Maria Bermons sent greetings; they were administrating the estate of William Gingee, who died intestate. The document discusses the funeral, creditors, and property, an accounting of which was to be complete by the end of October 1678. Signed by Marcus Cottle and Reglius Pinfold, Sr. Recorded 17 June 1678, by Jno. Washbourne. (p. 157)

INDEX

ABBOT, Doctor 8
ABUT, Jno 29 47
ACCOMAC viii
ACCOMODATIONS 98
ACH, Jno 98
ADBURY, Chris 47
ADDISON, Alexdr 28 50
ADKINS, Robt 33
ADMIRAL (ship) 87
AIEREW, Jno 47
AILLWORTH, Wm 29 47 97
AILY, Joseph 4
AIRES, Benjamin ix 90 105; John 113; Mary 34
ALBY, Wm 28
ALCOHOL 8 45 60 95 98
ALEWORTH, Darkas 99; Darkes 99; Will xiii 110;
ALLEN, Ed 46; Edmd 29 36 38
ALLISON, Edward 31
ALLSOP, Jno 2
ALTERCATIONS 45
AMES, Joseph 27
AMMUNITION 9 77
ANDERSON, Jno 44 55 63 70, 116; John 62 83 93 104; Teage 47; Teige 50; William 67 80 83 90 93 105 116; Wm 2 4 5 8 12 14 16 18 23 29 33 35-39 43 44 47 52 55 62 65 66 71 72 77 80 81 83 86 89 115 116 117
ANDREWES, Teage 29
ANDREWS, Will 76; Wm 8
ANOUGHTON, Wm 47
APPLE TREES 107
AQUIA CREEK v
ARCHBOLD, George 3
ARCHEBOLD, George 17
ARCHER, Jno 3
ARES, Jno 30

ARMESTRONG, Henry 30
ARMSTRONG, Henry 23 33-35 41 42
ARRISKIN, Wm 11 18
ARTHUR (Indian) xiv 99
ARUE, Jno 30
ASHBY, Ed 88; Edwd 107; Mr 115
ASSAULT ix 19 41 45 62 64 65 71 81 82 90
ASSEWOMAN 41
ATEAGE, Lau 49
ATKINS, James 27; Jno 47; Robert 84
ATKINSON, James 50 64 88 98; Robt 48 81 87; Saml 50
ATTEAGE, Laurence 28
AVERY, Mr 116
BACON, Dan 54; Jno xvi 42 43; Nath 31; Nathaniel v vi; Thomas v
BACON'S REBELLION v - viii x xiii xvi 31 44 50 51 54 56 68 69 85 91 96
BACY, Tho 2
BAGWELL, Jno 5 25 29 46 81 100; John 62 95; Tho 25 29 46 116; Thomas 59 89 116
BAKER, John xv 61
BALLARD, Mary 41 65 70
BALLY, Mr 2 11 13 23 40 41 51 55 100 112 116; Rich 11 13 16 22 31 39 49 52 57; Richard 1 5 10 13 17 21 25-27 32 35 37 39 42 46 52 55 57 62 63 80 85 103 109 114; Richd 42; Tho 8
BARBADOS 7
BARKE, Jno 48
BARKER, Jno 17 25; Roger 28 50

BARKS, Jno 29
BARNES, Frans 42; Henry 6 97; Jno 11 48 81 100 114; John 96; Thomas 58
BARNET, Jno 28 49; Jno Jr 19; John 113; Tho 49 79 101; Thom 116; Thomas xvii 77 100 107 115
BARRET, Tho 14 54 56 67; Thomas 59
BARRIFF, Thomas 43
BARRIMORE, Tho 5
BARRIT, Tho 5 48 52 66
BARTON, Tho 28 49
BASENT, Tho 47
BASTARD BEARING 32 34 41 43 63 64 65 67 70 99 113
BAYLY, Ann Jr 95; Katherin 17; Richard 95
BEACH, Samuel 101
BEARS xi 62
BEDAR, Wm 22
BEECH, Samuel 46; Sara 101
BELL, George 49; Mary 64; Tho 13 40; Tho Jr 28; Tho Sr 50
BELLMAINE, Jno 42
BELLMAME, Jno 17
BELLMAN, Jno 25
BELMAINE, Jno 71
BELMAN, Jno 82
BENCE, Canutus 52 88; Cornutus 48 91
BENGOR, Ellioner 54
BENSTON, Rebeca 24; Rebecca xi 24 59; Wm 24 30 48
BERKELEY, Governor vi vii xvi; William viii 9 20 21 33 68; Wm vi 23 24 31 56
BERKELY, William 9; Wm 31 52 56

BERMONS, Maria 117
BERN, Jenet 33
BERNHAM, Roger 30
BERRET, Tho 30
BESENT, Thomas 109
BEST, Dr 111; Jno 110; John xiii 100 110
BETTS, Elizabeth 103; Jno 15 21 95; John 103
BIRD, Edward 28
BIRRIT, Tho 1
BISHOP, John 69
BLACK, Tho 30
BLACKLOCK, Christian 34; Mr 10 14; Tho 5 52; Tho Sr 30
BLAKE, Thomas 98; Wm 30 48 50 84 87
BLAND, Samuel 25
BLOCKSON, Jno 5
BLOMEFEILD, Wm 17
BLOXUM, Jno 30
BOAT, Anna 92; Mrs 43
BOATE, Ann 4 12; Anna 33; Mrs 4 25
BOATS vii xi xviii 23 63 113
BOICE, George xiii xiv 41 44 45
BOILES, Danl 13
BOISE, George 37 46; Tho 34; Thomas 21
BONEWELL, James 29
BONVILL, Amos 14
BOOTH, James 48; Jno 28 50
BOOTY, Peter xvi 34
BORRICK, Jno 42
BOTE, Anna 43 104
BOUGHERTY, Nathan 86
BOUM, Wm 41
BOUNTIES xi
BOUROWS, Thomas 84
BOWEN, Jno 30 48; John 87
BOWIN, Jno 87; John 87

BOWMAN, Edm xiv 2 26 34 42 43 46 55-57 61-65 67 68 71 72 77 79 83-85 88 90 93 94 98 99 103 108 111 112; Edmd 7 9 18 29 32 33 35 40 41 47 106 109 111 114; Edmond 34 41 42 46 98 99; Edmund 95; Elinor xiv xv 46; Ellinor 34; Maj 20 40 42 47 58 63 64 83 98 99 111; Mrs 20
BOYCE, George 45
BOYES, Geo 44; George xiii 44
BOYLE, Mr 20
BOYSE, George 44
BRACY, Robt 8 9 12 30 79 87
BRACYE, Robert 1
BRADFORD, Henry 12 27; Mr 111; Nath 7 8 12 29 46 72 80; Nathan 38 66; Nathaniel x xi xvii xviii 26 62 66 80 85 86 91 93 94 97 98 100 101-103 107 108; Nathanl 23 64 86 101; Nathl 75 79
BRAMAL, Henry 84
BRAMBLE, Henry 28
BRAMUL, Henry 85
BREADERTON, Edward 30
BRICKHILL, Joseph 2
BRICKHOUS, George 17
BRICKHOUSE, Georg 28; George 1 49
BRICKS 77
BRIDGES 57
BRIGGS, Mary 92; Robert 92
BRIGHTINGHAM, Wm 48
BRIGHTINHAM, Wm 30
BRIGS, Mary 92
BRISTOL, ENGLAND xvi 9 17 42

BROADE, Jane xii 99
BROCKS, Jno 30
BROKE, Jane 9
BROMELY, Thomas 10
BROOKES, Francis 76; Henry 76; Jane 9; Jno 8 9 47; John 9
BROOKS, Jno 1 5
BROTHERTON, Ed 104; Edward 41 47 68 100
BROWN, An 34; Mr 13, 23; Peter 110; Tabitha 10 14 17 22; Tho 1 22
BROWNE, Ann 34; Devorax 14; Mrs 22; Peter 40 110; Tab 28; Tabitha 32 46 56 77 85 90 96 112; Tho 11 18 21 25 28 49 50; Thomas viii 1; Wm 30 47 91
BULL, Tob 48; Tobby 8; Tobias 97 109
BUNDICK, Rich 47; Rich Jr 47; Richard 19; Richard Sr 18 20
BUNDICK (Indian) 76
BUNDOCK, Rich 29; Rich Sr 29; Richard Sr 70 78
BURCH, Jno 33
BURD, Edwd 49
BURNESIDE, Wm 35
BURNESIDES, Wm 43 53
BURNSIDES, Wm 43
BURNTSIDES, Wm 61
BUROUGS, John 81
BURROS, Thomas 91
BURROWES, Tho 47; Thomas 84
BURT, Jno 28
BURTON, Robert 19; Robt 29 47; Tho 5; William xvii 101 102; Wm 10 29 46 59 86 91 100 103 116
BUSHALL, Tho 2 11 27;

BUSHALL (continued)
    Thomas xiii 26
BUSHELL, Tho 49
BUSHOP, Jno 46
BYLES, Daniel 28; Danl 50
CABLE, Elizabeth 95
CALENDAR xix
CALVERT, Charles 29; Christopher Sr 76; Xophr 29
CAMELL, James 33
CANADY, Margret 88
CARE, Jno 1
CAREE, Jno 47
CARTER, Edward 30; Grace 112; Jno 30; Paul 29 47 79; Pawl vii 51
CATHOLICS xvi
CATTLE xvii 6 7 17 24 35 41 51 52 55 56 60 62 66 70 76 78 84 86 91 100 102 107
CHACE, William xv 75 91-93 104 115; Wm 10 20 35 37 38 49 93 95
CHALLTON, Ann 76
CHAMBERS, Frances 95
CHANCY, Henry 15 16 29 47
CHAPELL, Mary 69; Tho 69
CHAPMAN, James 97
CHAPPEL, Mary 69; Thomas 69
CHAPPELL, Tho 70 75
CHAPWELL, Mary xv 53 69; Tho 50 53; Thomas xv
CHARLES, Jno vii 44 97
CHARLES CITY v
CHARLETON, Ann 49 54 78; Mrs ix 28 40 45
CHARNOCK, George 27 49 80 81 94 100 108
CHARNOK, George 4
CHARNOKE, George 4
CHASE, Wm 4
CHESAPEAKE BAY vi

CHESINESSICKS 42
CHILDREN 40 41 51 53 55 61 63-65 67 76 78 86
CHRISTMAS 101
CHURCH xiii xvi 16 58 63 64 67 70 76 95
CHURCH PATH 97
CIDER 112
CLARKE, John 86; Joseph 28 48; Tho 46
CLAVILL, Peter 30 47; Petr 95
CLAYTON, Mr 100 111 113; Tho 107 110 112
CLEARKE, Jno 87
CLIFFEN, Thomas 89 96
CLIFFON, Tho 30 48 50; Thomas 99
CLIFTON, Hannah 104; Tho 26; Thomas xvi 95
CLOTHING 22
COALE, Jno 2 4 5 7 8 11 15-17 20 22 24 26 32 35 37 40 41 44 51 52
COB, Jno 53 60
COBB, Wm 28
COCK, Tho 40 111; Thomas 110
COCKS, Thomas 110
COE, Timo 48; Timothy vii xvi 30 41 51 97
COKES, Richard 82
COLBURNE, Wm 2 12
COLE, Jno 15-17 25 27 39 43 45 49 51-54 61 81 95 109 112; John vii xiv xv 61 63 64 72 77 83 84 88-91 96 99 104 108 109
COLE'S TAVERN vii x xvi
COLLENON, Owen 27
COLLINS, Jno 69; John 96; Wm 3 8 45
COLLISON, James 1 25;

COLLISON (continued)
　　Mr 8
COLLONEL, Owen 3
COLLONELL, Owen 5 8
COLLONEN, Owen 48
COLVERT, Charles 47
COOK, Jno 7
COOKE, Japhet 27 64 77 78
　　85; Jno 2
COOPER, Margret 42; Mr
　　115; Rich 54; Sa 112 117;
　　Samll 113 114 116; Samuel
　　xii 115
COPE, Giles 5 28 50 53 60
CORE, Jno 49
CORN 14 73 88
CORNELISON, Andrew 28
CORNELIUS, Andrew 15
CORR, Jno 28
COSTEN, Rich 46
COTTLE, Marcus 117
COTTON v
COULSTON, Ann xv 10; Jno
　　65; John 91
COURTHOUSE vii 58 60 77
　　117
COWDREY, Wm 8
COWDRY, Wm 12
COX, Rich 81 82
CRABB, William 106
CRABTREE, Jno 31, 42
CRICHILL, Saml 30
CROPIER, Jno 10 14 44 54
CROPPER, Eliz 55; Jno 27 45
　　51 55-57 62 65 72 73 75 87
　　93; John xv - xvii 55 61 65
　　70 73-75 79-81 87 91 92
CROPPIER, Jno 49
CULPEPER, Jno 6 8-10 55 58
　　76; Mary 58
CUMBERS, Ursula 37 38
CURLES v
CURY, Jno 30

CUSTIS, Capt 13 17 19 23 38
　　39 79 98; Gen 86; Henry
　　76 94; Jno 3 14 71 75 84
　　85 106 108 110 112; John
　　vi viii xiv 71 86; Maj Gen
　　40 112; Mr 2 51; Robt 14;
　　William xvii 63 94 95 103
　　108; Wm 6 9 10 18 21-26
　　29 31 32 35 37 38 39 46 50
　　57 61 62 66 68 71 72 79 84
　　85 88 109 114 116
CUTLER, Rich 21 29 47
CUTTIN, Wm 49
CUTTING, Wm 28
DANIEL, Owen 29
DARBIE, Daniel 92
DARBY, Danl 27 49
DAVINSON, David 99
DAVIS, Evan 30 34 35 42 48
　　87 91; George 71; Jno 65
　　68 108; John 68 105; Robert 96; Robt 30; Tho 54
DE VRON (?) 8
DEEP CREEK 109
DEEP CREEK MILL 6 38
DEFAMATION x 20 54 65
DELASTATIS, Soustian 68
DENNIS, Morris 30 52
DERBY, Danl 50
DERRICK, Henry 9
DEVENISH, Jno 49
DEWELLS, Morg 49
DEWY, George 7
DICK (Indian) xiv 98
DICK (Negro) 54
DINE, Wm 48
DISTURBANCES x
DITON, Jane 20 99
DIX, Isaac 3 5; Isaack 47;
　　Isack 30; Issaack 21
DOBBINS, Mary 54
DOBINS, Mary 18
DOCTORS 110 111

DOE, Ralph 5 28 81 87 91 92
DOLBY, Edw 25; Edward 5 25 28; Jno 28 49; Peter 53 54 100 102
DORTHION, Roger 55
DORTON, Abraham 27 34
DOTHERTY, Nath 30
DOWMAN, Jno 21 54
DRAPER, Alexander 53 80
DRUMMOND, Jno 93; John 88
DRUMOND, Jno 10 30 48 52 58 67; John 57 84; Mr 63; Patience 34
DRUNKENNESS 72
DUE, George 12 50
DUELL, Thomas 96
DUGUIS, Robt 48
DUN, Alexander xiv 45 63
DUNBARR, Robt 42
DUNGWORTH, Robt 82
DUNN, Alex 46; Nich 97
DUPPER, Ann 97
DUY, George 28
DYNE, Wm 27
DYTON, Jane 17 20 21
E., Margaret 55
EBORNE, Ann 69 70 79; Henry 69; Mary xv xviii 40; Rebecca 69 78; Sara 53 69 86; Sarah xv xviii; Sarha 40; William xv 102; Wm 53 60 69 70 78 79
EBOURNE, Sara 86
ECONOMY xi
EDGE, Thomas x 117
EDMNDS, Owen 8
EDWAR (sic) REVELL'S BRIDGE 6
EDWARD HAMOND'S BRANCH 109
EDWARDS, Mordy 49; Nicholas 1
ELECTIONS 65
ELLIOT, Jno 2
EMONT, Wm 52
EMOT, Wm 2
ENGLAND 7
ESHAM, Danl 28 49
EUELL, James x 101 117
EVAN, Jno 48
EVANS, Jno 30 113; Thomas vii 69
EVERY, Mr 116
EWEL, James xvii 66
EWELL, An 16; Ann 16 62; James 16 29 37 62 66 77 86 91 101 104 107 108; Jams 16
EYR, Ben 113
EYRE, Ben 68 71 83 88 90 91 93 99 109 110 112 113 115 116; Benj 87; Benja 68
FAIRFAX, James 96
FARSY, Munsly 1
FAUSET, John 110; Mrs 27; Rhody 4; Wm 54 73 75
FAUSIT, Rodia 91
FAWSET, Jno 54; John xix 56 65 110; Rhodia 54; Rhody xv 51 65; Rodeah 110; Rodiah 110; Rody 5; William xv xix; Wm 51 65 73 75
FEILD, Jno 28; Thomas 83
FENN, Jno 10 14 21 29 47
FILBY, Stephen 113
FINLOW, Mary 34
FISHER, Phill 28 49; Phillip 21 76 106
FITTIMAN, Samuel 105
FLACK, Jno 17 20
FLETCHER, Wiliam 44; Wm 7 14 27 40 45
FLOARD, George 17
FLOWER, Wm 97

FOOD xii 51 56 73 101
FOOKES, Tho 21
FORNICATION xv 41 63-65 67 70 95
FOSCUE, Simon 50
FOSSET, Charles 73; Mrs 74; Wm 73
FOSTER, Armsten 37; James 55; Munston 28; Vrmston 49 76
FOWKES, Amy 80; James 29 42 47; Tho 47 50
FOWKS, James 5; Tho 1
FOX, Ann 73 74 91
FOXCROFT, Capt 41; Isaak 51; Issack 40; Mr vi; Simon Sr 8
FRAME, Arth 30; Arthur ix 48 69 78 87 90
FRANCISCO, Jno 30 48
FRANKLIN, Jno 95; John 92; Rich 46; Richard 29 66
FRANKLING, John 89; Jone 62; Rich 66; Richard 66
FREANX (ketch) 63
FREEMAN, William vii 62 77 103; Wm 13 21 29 100
FREESTONE-HALL v
FRENCHMAN, Jno 49
FUNERALS xii 106 117
FURNIS, Sarah 95
FURNISHINGS 41 87
GARGANIS, Ellias 47
GARGAPHIA xvii 6 24 109 115
GARMAN, Wm 95 100
GARRISON, Rich 50
GARRITSON, Rich 29
GAUL, Arth 47
GENGOTEIGE 60
GERMAME, Wm 48
GERMAN, Wm 6 86 87
GIBBINS, David 8

GIBBON, David 19
GIBBONS, David 27 49; Henry 17 25
GIBSON, Alex 81; Alexander ix 4 64 71 81 82; Alexder 64; Laurence 1; Marck 1
GILL, Tho 23
GILLET, German 24
GIN, George 27; Jane 19
GINGEE, Capt 111; Joan 104 108 111 112; Joane 104 105; Joanna 117; Sebast 111 112; Sebastian 104 105 108; Sebastn 112; William 104 105 117; Wm 8 9 18 22 35-37 39 40 53 104 105 108 111 112
GINN, George 49
GIPSON, Alex 82
GITTINGS, Tho 28; Thomas 64 72
GLADING, Howel 30 47 109; Howell 95 98
GLEW, Saml 28
GLUE, Saml 49
GONSALVES, Jno 29
GONSOLVOS, Jno 47
GOODEING, Thomas 84 115
GOODING, Thomas 74
GOODMAN, Jno 49; Jon 56
GORDIN, Jno 50
GORDING, Tho 83
GORE, Max 27 48 74 75 92 100 113; Maxamilln 92; Maxamn 91; Maximilian 82; Maximillian 100; Maxlln 92
GOREING, Jno 28
GOSSLING, Elizabet 4; Elizabeth 5
GOULDING, William xvi; Wm 11
GOVERNOR v vi viii x 9 10

GOVERNOR (continued)
    16 20 21 23 24 31 32 33 38
    39 56 57 60 67 68 71 94 97
    105
GRAY, James 98
GREEN, Jno 49; Joseph 4
GREENE, Jno 28
GREGORY, Jacob 29
GREY, Miles 3
GROSSERS ADVENTURE
    (ship) xii 106
GRUBBING HOE (Indian) 72
GUNBY, Francis 115
GUNS 39 75 101 103 109
GUY, James 44 55 62 63 70
    83 93
HACK, Geo Nich 28 37 59 81
    91 104; Geo Nick 49;
    George 10; George Nich 25
    36; George Nichol 12;
    George Nicholas 8; George
    Nickolas 6 21
HACKS, George Nich 22
HALBE, Tho 95
HALL, Emanel 28; Eml 49;
    Tho xvii 6 25 27 49 73 74
    86; Thomas xvi xvii 61 72
    73 78 87; Wm 18 54
HAMERING, Jno 28
HAMMOND, Edward 52
HAMOND, Edward xi 1 7 10
    23 29 44 74 76 90 96 110;
    Edwd 4
HAMONDS, Edward 109
HANCOCK, Jno 47; John 79
HANCOK, Jno Jr 30
HANGER, Phill 45; Phillip 11
    40 110
HANMER, John 97
HANNING, Jno x 1 5 16 47
    81; John 109
HANSON, Jno xviii 4 12-15
    18 19 35 36 44 102;

HANSON (continued)
    John 60 108 115; Mr 45
HARCORT, Daniel 112
HARDER, Warrn 48
HARDY, Robert 78
HARMER, Jno 54
HARMOR, John 93
HARRIS, Jno 11 12 19 27
HARRISON, James 8 33 36
HARROT, Daniel 112
HARTWELL, Hen 9
HASELWOOD, Jno 81
HASTING, Rich 48
HAWES, Jno 59 72
HAZARD, Edward 80
HEDGES, Tho 19 48 54;
    Thomas 54
HENRICO COUNTY v
HENRY, Walter 83
HEUSE, James 42
HEWIT, Mikell 89
HICHIN, Edwd 48
HICKMAN, Wm 29
HILL, Capt 6 33 42 47 58 61
    89 97 99; Jacob 41; James
    14 15; Margret 41 64 97;
    Marie 34; Mary 41; Rich
    10 11 13 16 26 27 32 38
    58; Richard 1 2 5 25 32 34
    42 46 48 57 59 62 85 94 95
    109; Richd 73 93; Robert
    68; Robt 29 47
HINDERSON, Gilbert xv
    xviii; Gilbt xviii; Jon xv
    xviii 69
HINMAN, Rich 29 48; Richard 32
HOGBEN, Jno 18 20 27 83
    99; John 62
HOGS xvii 3 65 113
HOLAND, Rich 107
HOLDEN, Ch 14 16 34 43 44
    102; Cha 52 80;

HOLDEN (continued)
  Charles 16 53 68 71 72 79-81 86 93 99 108; Charls 3-5; Jno 49 101; John 101; Mary 101 107
HOLLAND, Rich 6 29 48 100; Richard xvii 27 77 115; Richd 101
HOLLIDAY, Joseph 107; Robt 36 38 89
HOLLIWELL, Rebecca 113
HOPKINS, Mr 115; Samll 115 116
HOREKEAL 116
HORNSBY, Jno 98
HORSES 7 14 20 39 56 60 70 73 76 78 86 87 115
HOULDING, Cha 80
HOUSEHOLD ITEMS xii 60
HOUSES 107 113
HOWERD, Elizabeth 42
HUCHINSON, John 90; Mr 21 45; Robert xiv 97 111; Robt 1 2 4 8 10 12 14 15 23 26 28 32 37 41 49 59 64 75 87 111-113 114
HUDSON, Robt 27 49
HUES, Edward 80
HUGES, Edward 17
HUHIN, Edward 29
HUIT, Michol 48 90; Rob 34; Robert xiii; Robt 26 27 37 90
HUNGAR'S PARISH 6 11 38
HUTCHINSON, Robert 7; Robt 8
ILLNESSES xii xiii 61 111
INDIANS v xi xiii xiv 45 46 62 65 68 72 75 76 79 98 99 112
JACKEIL, Joseph xii 106
JACKEILL, Joseph xii 106
JACKSON, Jona 81;

JACKSON (continued)
  Jonah 42 81; Jonas 50; Jonha 28; Owen 56 91
JACOB, Isaack 28
JAMES, David 28 49
JAMES (Indian) xiv 45
JAMES CITY 9 56
JAMES RIVER v
JAMES TOWN 94 113
JAMESTOWN v vi vii
JARMAN, Wm 30
JAUNSBY, Jno 98
JEFFREYES, Herbt 60
JEFFREYS, Herb 58 95 97 105; Herbert 57 94
JEFFRIES, Governor vii viii; Herbert 39; Tho 31
JELLSON, Edward 32 89
JENIFER, Capt 20 23 33 38 51; Daniel vi xvi xvii 3 21 24 26 35 38 39 41 42 57 67 71 72 74 82-84 104 110 111 112; Daniell 95 105; Danl 8 13 17 22 24 30 34 38 39 48 105
JENKINS, Henry 76; Jno 29; Jno Sr 47; John 84
JNOSON, George 9; Mr 100; Obed 11; Obedience 10 25
JOHNSON, George xvi 41 48 97 116; Jeptha 28 49; Jno 49; Mr 6 13 97 110; Netter 92; Obed 50 108; Obedience 1 21 22 26 28 32 38 40 57 95 98 103 109 110 111; Rich Sr 30 47; Richard Sr 56 67; Tho 6 8 28 50 64 81 95; Thomas 1 64
JOLLEY, Jno 45
JONES, Jno 29 46 58; Morgan 1; Rich Jr 79; Rich Sr 36; Richard 25; Richard Jr 99; Richard Sr ix 19 25;

JONES (continued)
    Tho xviii 4 13-15 18; Wm 27
JORDAIN, Dorothy 50
JOSEPH (servant) 73
JOYNES, Edmd 50; Edmond
    xv 28 69
JUSTICE, Ralph 25 87
KARTE, Rebecca 34
KELLUM, Jno 27; Rich 49;
    Richard 6 27; Richard Sr
    41 51 65 75 100
KELLY, Edm 8; Edmd 28 49
    50; Edmond 32
KENDALL, Col 54; William
    vi; Wm vii 9 14 67
KENNET, Wm 30 48
KENNETT, Wm 8
KEYES, Alice 97
KING 31 32 50 54 56 68 94
KING ROBIN 75 79
KIRKMAN, Roger 28 49
KNIGHT, Mary 41; Rebecca
    41 65 70
LATTIMORE, Jno 1
LAURENCE, Mary xiv 11;
    Nich 28; Nicholas xiv 11
LAW, Rich 29
LAWES, Jno 15 16 47; Jno Sr
    30
LAYLER, Nich 28 50
LEATHERBERY, Perry 21
LEATHERBURY, Charles 46
    47 50 76 99 115; Charls
    46; Elinor xiv xv 46; Peary
    46; Perry 99
LECAT, James 103; Jno 15
    37 49 103
LECATT, Jno xviii 14 15 27;
    John 103
LEGEAT, Jno 113
LEHHAM, Jno 27
LEWIS, Jno 2 29 47; Jno Sr
    47; Lucretia 34; Wm 19

LIMEGER, Joseph 33
LINEGER, Joseph 39 68
LINNEGER, Joseph 39
LIQUOR xi xii 60 114
LITTLETON, Capt 2 3 9 13
    15-18 25; Col vi 23 52 55
    56 58 69 70 75 77 82 85 91
    98 99 103 104; S 16 83 92
    94 116; So 27 31 46; Sou
    23 65 94 108; South 72;
    Southy vii x xvii 1 3 5-7
    9-11 13 15 17 18 20 21 22
    25 26 38 39 42 49 50 52 54
    56 57 61-63 65 66 67 68 71
    72 75 77-79 85 88 90 91
    93-95 97 98 105 106 108
    114 116
LOAME, Elizabeth 34
LONDON 9 39 81
LONGO, James 27 49
LORD, Frans 55 58 75
LOWEN, Wm 30
LOWING, William 39
LURTON, Henry 28 49
MACIN, Eliz 65
MACKELAMNY, Onny 48
MACKLAMIE, Eleanor 34
MACKLOME, Wonni 30
MACKWILLIAM, Finlow 48
MACKWILLIAMS, Finlow
    30
MACOME, Jno 48
MADDER, Xophr 49
MADDUX, Tho 28 44
MADUX, Tho 36 49; Thomas
    36
MAGISTRATES viii 71
MAJOR, Wm 6 14 27 49
MAKARTY, Daniel 85
MAKERTY, Daniel 85
MAN, Eliz 65; Elizabeth xvi
    34 41 43 68 100
MARAINER, Jno 27

INDEX

MARRIAGE xiv 107
MARSH, Owen 7
MARSHALL, Ann 34; Tho 28 50
MARTIAL, Wm 81
MARTIALL, William 62 90; Wm 3 4 21 29 45 47 87
MARTIN, Edward 27
MARVELL, Jno 48
MARVILL, Jno 30
MARYLAND xv 60 65 92 104
MASON, Nathaniel 32 85; Robert 96; Robt 30 47
MASONGO 97
MASSETEAGE 65
MASSETEAGE (Indian) ix
MASSY, Allexdr 48
MATAHOWS (Indian) 76
MATAPANY 39
MATCHEPUNGO 66
MATHEWS, Henry 102
MATTOX, Tho 8
MATTS, James 29 47 70 88 96 103 105-107 108 110; Mr 41
MEARES, Ann 42; Bar 81; Barth 46 88 100; Bartho 91; Barthol 87; Bartholemew 21 99 100
MEDCALFE, Isaack 29 46
MEDICAL CARE xiii 26 44 110 111
MEERES, Ann 4; Barth 29; Bartholemew 32
MELICCHOP, Nicholas 113
MELTON, Rich 49
METCALFE, Isaac 91
MICHAEL, Jno Jr 82
MICKAEL, Jno. Sr 10
MICKELL, Teage 30
MIDDLETON, George 47; Jno 8

MIDLETON, George 30; Jno 22
MIKAEL, Jno 76; Jno Sr 58; Mary 58
MIKEL, Roger 59
MIKELL, Jno 6 28 76; Jno Jr 2 49 52; Jno Sr 2 3 5 13 55; Jno. Sr 8; Roger 6 8 25 29 36 40 47 59 74
MILBURNE, John 82
MILES, Roger xiv 30 48 95 99
MILLBY, Jno 49 50
MILLECHOP, Nic 35 71; Nich 48 72; Nicho 30; Nicholas 23 34 35 42 113
MILLING, Jno 52
MILLSON, Jno 48
MISKELL, Teage 47
MITTS, James 75
MOCCARTY, Daniel 79
MONFORD, Tho 29
MOORE, Ed Sr 50; Edward Jr 97; Jno 33 48
MORGAN, Bridget 32; Peter 30; Tho 10 14; Wm x 13 24
MORGIN, Petr 48
MORINFORD, Tho 46
MORRIS, Dennis 30 48; Tho 47
MOTTS, Jno 9
MR. REVELL'S BRIDGE 38
MUDDY CREEK 109
MUKERELL, Lancelot 32
MURFRY, Owen 8
NAMES xviii
NANDUA 39
NANDUY CREEK xviii 14
NEGROES xi 7 29 30
NELLSON, Jno 30 49
NELSON, Jno 27
NEW KENT COUNTY v vi

NEWBOLD, Mr 117; Tho 3 117
NEWELL, Jno 116; John 89 115
NEWTON, Joseph 4 34
NIBLET, Rich 27 50 100; Richard 48
NICHOLES, Rich 31
NICKOWANSIN xvii 101
NIXSON, Tho 48 87 116; Thomas 116
NOCK, William 96; Wm 7 17 29 31 46 81 86 98 107
NORRIS, James 42
NORTHAMPTON COUNTY 67
NORTON, Wm 30 84
NUBOLD, Mr 116; Tho 3 30 48 53
NUCOMB, Paptis 47
NUCOMES, Thomas 18
NUMAN, Nicholas 25
NUTON, Joseph xv 27 29 40 47 53 69 72
OATES, Martin 29
OBEN, Ann 6
OCAHONE, Jone viii 23 24; Phillip viii 23 24
OCCACONSON INDIANS 68
OCCAHANNOCK 38 109
OCCAHANOCK 6
OCCAHONE, Phill 24; Phillip 24
OCCASONSON ix 65
OGRAYHAN, Danl 49
OLIVER, Dorothy 17; Saml 30; Vincent 97
ONANCOCK 29 38
ONELY, Clemt 48
ONOUGHTON, Wm 83
ONYONS, Jno 30
OSBURNE, Tho 48 81-83 86; Thomas 87 88 105

OTTERS, Mart 47
OWEN, Barbery xvii 101; Daniel 82 85; Danl 29; Ince 95; Jnothn 48; Jon 86; Jonath 6; Jonathan 1 13 78 87; Jonathen 30; Rich 97
OWIN, Daniel 86 91 101; Jnoath 87
PAINTER, Richard viii 22 29; Sarah viii 22
PAKES, Charles 46
PALMER, Edwd 18
PANTHERS 62
PARKE, Henry xii 88 96 106 107
PARKER, George 75; Jno 32 36 37 39 40 47 99; Jon 29; Peter 29 47 50 67 100 106; William 62; Wm 29 47 50 59
PARKES, Charles 55 64 65; Hen 54; Jno 50 53 60
PARKS, Jno 14 28
PARRAMORE, Tho 60; Widow 28
PARRIMORE, Mary 50; Tho 28 50
PARSONS, Jno 14 30 47
PASH, Jno 52
PATTISON, George 53
PEACOCK, Elizabeth 41 63
PEALE, Robt 28
PEARSE, Davis 81
PECO, Peter 82 105
PECOE, Peter 83 88
PECOEH, Peter 83
PEIRCE, Jno 14
PEROFRANK, Jno 42
PHILBIE, Stephen 113
PHILLBY, Stephan 47; Stephen 114
PIGS 76 84 86 100
PILSWORTH, Mr 106

INDEX

PINFOLD, Reglius Sr 117
PITTMAN, Jos 50; Joseph 28
PIWELL, Rich 29 100; Richard 76 96
POCOMOCK 83
POCOMOKE 115
POKEAMOKE 115
POKEHETENORTON 73
POKOMOKE 6
POMERAY, Saml 17
POOLE, Elizabeth 98
POPE, Mathew 4; Thomas 21
POWELL, Redrick 28; Rhed 49; Rho 52; Rhodrick 81
PRETTIMAN, Jno 6 47; Jno Jr 28; John 97; Wm 30
PRICE, Rich 70 73; Richard xvi xvii 25 73 74 87
PRICHARD, Peter 29 47
PRIER, James 93
PRIEST, George 17
PRITCHET, Peter xi 106
PROFANITY 94
PRYER, James 93
PUNGETEAG CHURCH 111
PUNGOTEAG 83
PUNGOTEAGE vii xi xiii 38 58 77
PUNGOTEEG 112
PUNGOTEGE 113
QUAKERS xvi 41
QUINTON, Phill 47; Phillip 84
RAHAN, Edwd 48
RAINY, James 53 94 104; Jno 53 97; John 91 113
RAMEY, Jno 105
RAPPAHONOCKECOUNTY 81
RATCLIFE, Nath 33
RATCLIFF, Charles 30; Nath 48
READ, Hen 100;

READ (continued)
  Henry x 12 16 25; Jno 28 79; Walter 93 104
READE, Henry vii xiii 16 21 27 44 49 76 87; John 69 70; Jone 44
READS, Joan 38
REEVES, Jno 12 26 101
REGAN, Darby 47
REGON, Darby 29
RELIGION xvi
RENNIE, Jno 60
RENNY, James 61 75 79 104; Jno 30 48 50 53 61 79 86; John 80
REVEL, Edw 11; Edwd 14; Mr 38
REVELL, Edward x 14 29 46 57 71 93 110; Edwd 14; John 81; Mr 8 109
REVELL'S BRIDGE 109
REVES, Jno 101
REYDON, Margret 41
RICHARDS, Rich 109; Richard 109
RICHARDSON, David 8; Robert 106
RICKMAN, Margret 41 63
RIDING, Mr 6 22 23 33; Tho 3 10 11 25 32 36; Thomas viii
ROADS 57 59
ROBERTS, Charles 42; Francis 28; Frans 51; Frans. 41; Fras 50; Xophr 48
ROBIN, King 75 79
ROBINS, Arth 31 60; Arthr 27 50; Arthur 7 8 18 38 42 53 55 60 69 70 78 79 102 108 115; Frans 31; Mr 38
ROBINSON, Adam 30; Elizbeth 13; Max 81
RODGERS, Henry 30

ROE, George 49
ROGERS, Hen 48; Jno 35;
　John 107; Nich 25 35;
　Nicholas 20 43; Reuth 42;
　Thomas 89
ROLPH, Tho 54; Thoms 18
ROWLES, Jno 8 27 49 116;
　John 116
RUNAWAY SERVANTS 73
　74
RUSSELL, George ix 16 45
RUST, Jno 27
RYCON, Margt 65
RYDING, Tho 22 28 38 49;
　Thom 50
RYDON, Margeret 67
RYLY, Tho 47
SABBATH xvi 41 95
SADBURY, Christopher x 29
　72 80; Mr 8; Sarah 12;
　Xopher 64 83 89; Xophr 80
SADDLES 77
SANDERS, Richard 42
SANDFORD, Mr 116; Samll
　114 115 117; Samuel xii
　113 115
SAUNDERS, Richard 4
SAVADGE, Jno 28 111
SAVAGE, Griff 16 26 41 47
　76; Griffeth 76; Griffin 29;
　Jno 10 14 21 32 33 50 87
　95; John 88; Mary 54; Row
　49; Rowland 18 27; Tho 28
SAVEDG, John 111
SCAMEL, Jno 20
SCAMELL, James 50; Jno 20
　28 49
SCARBROW, Mathew xvii 24
SCARBURGH, Capt 58 79;
　Ch 39; Cha 78 82; Charles
　vi viii x 10 29 32 33 39 47
　57 61 64 71 77 78 82 86 88
　95 104 109 113 116;

SCARBURGH (continued)
　Charls 3 11; Ed 23 40 48 80
　82; Edm ix 1 3 5 6 17-19 22
　23 57 68 70 77-79 84 88
　101; Edmd 7 10 19-22 27 32
　49 104 106 109; Edmond 38
　39 80 107 116; Edmund 57
　95; Henry 4; Mary 29
SCARBUROUGH, Mathew 7
SCARBUROW, Mathew 54
SCOT, Henry 28
SCOTCH BETTS 41
SELBY, Tobias 91
SELIVANT, Dennis 49
SELLIVANT, Dennis 28;
　Denns 50; Dormt 27
SELLMAN, Hen 102; Henry
　49 89 92 100 107
SELMAN, Hen 101; Henry
　27 100
SELVY, Elizabeth 10; Tob 10
　49; Tobias 10 14 27 93 97;
　Toby 4
SENIOR, James xii 106
SENNERS, Jno 5
SEPELL, Garatt 79
SERJEANT, Saml 49; Samuel
　27
SERVANTS xvi
SHARS, Solomon 2
SHEALE, Rich 28 49
SHELLE, Susanna 42
SHEPARD, Jno 1
SHEPPARD, Jno 28 50
SHERIFF xvi 2 6 8 9 13 16
　18 19 25 32 33 35-38 40-43
　53 54 55 61 62 64 65 67 70
　71 72 74 81 83 84 88 89 90
　93-97 104 105 108 110-112
　113 115
SHERRWOOD, Wm 7 15
SHIP, Mathew 6
SHIPP, Math 49;

SHIPP (continued)
  Mathew 27 43 64
SHIPS 14 17 50 51
SILL, Wm 71
SILVERTHORNE, William x 104 108 112; Wm 29 47 114
SIMONS, Will 79; Wm ix 19
SIMPSON, Jno 32
SMALLY, Jno 6 14 27; Tho 30
SMALPEECE, Tho 48
SMITH, Edward 25 71 76; Edwd 67; Eliz 52 67 71; Elizabeth 43 44 105; George 28 78; Jno xvi 1 6 28 42; Jno Jr 50; Jno Sr 50; Joice 85; Joshua 48; Josua 30; Rich 55; Richard 1; Simond 30; Wm 17 22 24 25 61
SOMERS, Jno 52; Margret 52
SOMERSET COUNTY 63 81 83
SOUTHERN, Richard 108
SOUTHERNE, Edward 116
SPENCER, Will 109; William 54 90 96 102 110; Wm 44 52 91
STANLY, Xopher 30; Xophr 50; Xopr 48
STEAPHANS, James 78
STEAVENS, James 19 28 70; Wm 45 115
STEENACRE, Cornelius 83
STEPHENSON, Jno 24; John xvii
STEVANS, James 19; Will 83; William xiii 44; Wm 21 44 49
STEVENS, Cornelius 88
STEVENSON, Walter 42
STOCKLY, Woodman 88

STOCKS 117
STOKELY, Frans 33; Jno 30 41 43 44 48 52 67 71 86 95; Jno Jr 61; Jno Sr 29 46; John 109; Mary 43 76 77; Tho 61; William 95; Wm 30 48; Wood 48; Woodman 30 59
STOKLY, John 95
STOPP, Andrew 47
STOTT, Andrew 29; Henrery 109; Henry 28 49
STRATTON, Elizabeth 13; Jno vii x 21 24 36 40 48 50 52 54 56 61 66 70 94 99; John xii 56 65 67 95 99
STRINGER, Col vi 11; Hillary 17 33 35 37 39 46 57 95 96; Jno 36 44
STURGES, Jno vii 30 51
STURGIS, Jno 47 59 96
SUFFOLK v
SUICIDE xvii 24
SULLIVANT, Dormt 48
SUPPLE, Garet 29; Garret 47 75 79 89 97; Garrt 95
SWAN, Alex 14; Alexander 3
SWANNE, Alexander 3
SYMMONS, Tom 48
SYMONS, Wm 19 85
TALBOT, Benedict 96
TANKARD, Jno 25 71 81 107 110 112; John 84 104 108 109; Mr 3-5 13 22 34 35 40 43 44 61 64 65 88 100 102
TANKRED, Mr 72
TANNER, Jno 81; John 91 92
TARR, Jno 13 48 70 81; John 75 78 84 87
TAXES 31 33
TAYLER, Abr 81; Abrah 49; Abraham 10 14 27 62; Debora 38;

TAYLER (continued)
  James 48 83 84 95; Jno 29
  47 86; John 82 85 93; Jone
  viii; Saml 16 48; Samuel 5
  21 22 34 39 68; Samul 6 30;
  Tho 29 95; Thomas 82; To
  47; Walter viii 23 47 79 80
  107; Wm 2; Wm Sr ix 30 48
  65 68
TEACKLE, Tho 70; Thomas 58
TEAGLE, Tho 49
TEAKLE, Tho 27 34 41 75; Thomas 13
TERNAN, Ann 34
TERNON, Roger 47
TERRY, Jno 46
THIEVERY xvii
THOMAS, Morgan 8 27 50 87; Morgin 4 48; Simon 26; Symon 26
THOMPSON, Christopher 56
THOMSON, Chr 30 86; Christopher xiv 48 67; Jno 18 28 49; Xopher 85 98; Xophr 86
THORNE, Joseph 12; Thomas 12
THORNTON, Patience xii 99
THORTON, Wm 48
THRIFT, Joan 97
TILGHMAN, Mary 88; Rich 88
TILLNEY, Jno 82
TILLNY, Jn 49; Jno 28 64 71 81
TILNEY, Jno 81 82; John ix
TILNY, Jno 64
TINLY, Jno 64
TITHABLES 6 27-30 33 38 57 109
TOULSEL 42
TOUNSEN, Jno 29
TOUNSEND, Jno 47
TRAFFICK, Wm 29
TRAFFORD, William 100; Wm 23
TRAFORD, Wm 46
TREWET, James 30
TRINNIMAN, Benjamen 10
TRUIT, Elisabeth 96; George 29 48; Henry 29; Jno 19
TRUITT, Henry 19
TRULACE (Negro) 55
TRUMAN, Jno 28 49
TUBBIN, Nich 28
TUBBINS, Nich 33 49; Nicholas 20
TUCK, James 29 53 61 79 90 93
TUCKFEILD, Saml 8
TURNER, Richard 76
TYER, Tho 90; Thomas 89
TYLER, Nich 49
TYRA, Tho 25 35
TYZAR, Tho 27
UELL, James 47 97 98
UPSHOT, Arthur 35 75 79 98 100 107; Authur 43
UPSHOTT, Mr 8
VAHUN, Edw 30
VANNETSON, Gueslin 30
VENETSON, Inquisn 48
WADDELOE, Nicholas 83
WAFERS, Jno 17
WAGAMAN, Hend 111 114; Hendrick x 112; Henrick 111 113
WAGGAMAN, Hend 28 49 95 104; Hendrick 4 5 10 21
WAILE, William 4
WAITE, Will 87; Wm 79
WALE, Wm 97
WALKER, James 29 46 50 86 91 94; Nath vii 50 51; Nathanl 51; Peter 30 39

WALKER (continued)
86; Petr 48; Tho 63
WALLIS, William 91 114;
Wm 48 114
WALLOP, Jno 1 6 10 11 13
16 22 25 26 30 31 32 35 37
38 39 42 43 48 50 52 57 59
60 65 77 97 98 103 106
107-109; John viii 63 70 95
106; Mr 23 41 63
WALTER, John 110
WALTERS, Mr 111
WALTHOM, Jno 48
WARREN, Steph 47
WARRINGTON, Steaphen 96;
Stephan 29 95; Steven 100
WARRWICK BAY 51
WARRWICKS CREEK BAY
vii 50
WASHBOURNE, Jno 7 9 12
16 17 20 21 24 38 39 42 46
51 58 60 67 80 93 95 106
117; John xviii 94 115
WATCHEPREGUE 80
WATERLAND, Capt 12;
Jonathan 115; Mary 42
WATHAN, James 63
WATHIN, James 63
WATS, Jno 110
WATSON, George 4; Petr 48;
Robert xiii; Robt 1 28 47
61 111; Robt Sr 29 50 53;
Sara 42
WATTS, Dorothy xi 59; Jno x
16 30 41 47 48 110 111;
John xiii 39 91 100 107
110; Jon 29
WATTS ISLAND 23 93
WAYT, Will 87
WEBB, Tho 16 29 47
WEBSTER, Jno 3; John xvii
WEILDING, Edward 32
WEINES, Morg 49

WELBORNE, Tho 5
WELBURN, Tho 65
WELBURNE, Jno 71 115; Mr
37 97 110 115; Tho 3 6 8 9
12 18 20 23 33 35 36 40 53
71 87 97; Thomas 19 68 71
79 97 98 105 106 108 114
115
WELBURNES, Thomas 97
WELCH, Rich 28 50
WELCHMAN, Jno 55
WELLS, Mary 95
WEST, Geo 95; George 30 41
47 81 82 86; Jno vii viii 2 3
5 8 11 15-17 20 21 23 26
29 43 46 47 51 54 55-57 59
61 64 71 72 75 76 80 81 84
86 93 96 98 104 114 116;
John x xi 62 63 67 68 72
75 79 84 88 89 92 94 95 96
104 116; Jon 93; Maj 2 3
13 15 55 68 78 80 86 89 92
93 95 97 99 100 108 110
116; Major 16; Mr 4; Robt
30
WHARTON, Fran 8 29; Frans
8 47 56
WHEELER, George 30; Tho
1
WHITE, Amb 2 3 7 29 38 47
61 62 65 82 84 88-90 104
108; Ambr 103; Ambrose
xi 1 68 71 82 83 89 92;
Ann 25; Jno 28 50; Mr 3
13 14 63 65; Richard 25
55; William 103; Wm 1 27
47 49 76
WHITTINGTON, William 53;
Wm 7 15 25 32 35 43 53
56 61 69 91
WHITTMAN, Stephan 27
WHOREKILL 116
WHRIGHT, Edward 36;

WHRIGHT (continued)
  William 107; Wm 28
WHYT, Ann 22
WILD ANIMALS 62
WILDCATS 62
WILLET, Wm 3 32
WILLIAM, Jno 55
WILLIAMS, Edward 17;
  Henry 29 46; Rich 17 48
  95; Richard 90 103; Seborn
  95; Tho 49 83; Thomas xvii
  xviii 94 95 101; Wm 27 50
  109
WILLIAMSON, Wm 32
WILLING MINDE (ship) 8
WILLIS, Jane 62 66; Jno 29
  46 66; John 62 66
WILLSON, Mary 88; Tho 2
  19 27; Wm 10 29 32 47
WILLY, Tho 59; Thomas 59
WINDHAM, Mary ix 40 45
  78
WINSEWACK (Indian) xiv 45
WINTER xviii;

WINTER (continued)
  Andrew xiii 26 34; Dr 26
WISE, Jno 9 11 15 31 32
  37-39 42 47 52 57; Jno Sr
  29; John viii 95; Mr 2 6
WM & ANN (ship) 42 69
WM & JOHN (ship) 17
WOLVES 8 62
WOOD, Rich 49
WOODCRAFT, Rich 55
WOODLAND, Joseph 65 73
  91
WOULDHASE, Wm 27
WOULDHAVE, Wm 49
WRIGHT, Edward 30 80
WYATT, Wm 70 87
WYER, Charles 106 110
YARDLY, Henry 8
YEO, Hugh 14 49 57; Wm 28
  49
YORKE, Peter 28 41 89 96
YOUEL, James 66
YOUELL, James 66
YOUNG, Jno 48

Other Heritage Books by JoAnn Riley McKey:

Accomack County, Virginia Court Order Abstracts, Volume 1: 1663–1666

Accomack County, Virginia Court Order Abstracts, Volume 2: 1666–1670

Accomack County, Virginia Court Order Abstracts, Volume 3: 1671–1673

Accomack County, Virginia Court Order Abstracts, Volume 4: 1673–1676

Accomack County, Virginia Court Order Abstracts, Volume 5: 1676–1678

Accomack County, Virginia Court Order Abstracts, Volume 6: 1678–1682

Accomack County, Virginia Court Order Abstracts, Volume 7: 1682–1690

Accomack County, Virginia Court Order Abstracts, Volume 8: 1690–1697

Accomack County, Virginia Court Order Abstracts, Volume 9: 1697–1703

Accomack County, Virginia Court Order Abstracts, Volume 10: 1703–1710

Accomack County, Virginia Court Order Abstracts, Volume 11: 1710–1714

Accomack County, Virginia Court Order Abstracts, Volumes 12 and 13: 1714–1719

Accomack County, Virginia Court Order Abstracts, Volume 14: 1719–1724

Accomack County, Virginia Court Order Abstracts, Volume 15: 1724–1731

Accomack County, Virginia Court Order Abstracts, Volume 16: 1731–1736

Accomack County, Virginia Court Order Abstracts, Volume 17: 1737–1744

CD: *Accomack County, Virginia Court Order Abstracts, Volumes 1–10: 1663–1710*

Baptismal Records of the Dutch Reformed Churches in the City of Groningen, Netherlands, Volume 1: 1640–1649

Baptismal Records of the Dutch Reformed Churches in the City of Groningen, Netherlands, Volume 2: 1650–1659

CD: *Baptismal Records of the Dutch Reformed Churches in the City of Groningen, Netherlands*

Wenches, Wives and Widows: Sixteen Women of Early Virginia

www.ingramcontent.com/pod-product-compliance
Lightning Source LLC
Chambersburg PA
CBHW050641160426
43194CB00010B/1758